PERMISSIVE IGNORANCE
*An Invitation to Examine and Discover the
Truth about Christianity*

Brian P. Marchionni

Ex Animo Press, Inc. • Franklin, Massachusetts

Permissive Ignorance
An Invitation to Examine and Discover the Truth about Christianity
By Brian P. Marchionni

Published by:
Ex Animo Press, Inc.
Suite 167
430 Franklin Village Drive
Franklin, MA 02038-4007
U.S.A.

orders@exanimopress.com
www.exanimopress.com

All rights reserved. No part of this book may be reproduced or transmitted in part or in whole by any means without express written consent from Ex Animo Press, Inc., except for brief quotations for a review.

© 2002 by Brian Marchionni

ISBN, print ed.   0-9721371-0-6
First printing 2002
Printed in the United States of America

Cover design: Peri Poloni, Knockout Design, Cameron Park, CA
www.knockoutbooks.com

Scripture taken from the HOLY BIBLE, NEW INTERNATIONAL VERSION®. Copyright © 1973, 1978, 1984 by International Bible Society. Used by permission of Zondervan. All rights reserved.

Publisher's Cataloging-in-Publication
(Provided by Quality Books, Inc.)

Marchionni, Brian P.
   Permissive ignorance : an invitation to examine and discover the truth about Christianity / Brian P. Marchionni. -- 1st ed.
   p. cm.
   ISBN 0-9721371-0-6

1. Christianity--Essence, genius, nature.
2. Apologetics--20th century.   I. Title.

BT60.M37 2003   230
                          QBI33-583

For my family.

Contents

✺

About the Author *6*
Foreword *7*
Introduction *9*

PART I - MOTIVATION

1. - Testimonial Number 19,948,342,644 15
2. - Strong Questions, Weak Answers 25
3. - Mythinformation 41
4. - Shady Characters 65
5. - Your Little Secrets 79
6. - All About Answers 95

PART II - RESOURCES

7. - Doing the Research 107

Epilogue *123*
Attributions *125*

ABOUT THE AUTHOR

Brian Marchionni would describe electrical engineering as his "day job." Outside of business hours, Brian likes to keep himself busy at The Church of the Nazarene at Trolley Square in Framingham, Massachusetts, in which capacity he maintains the church web site, helps to lead weekly worship, and assists in teaching weekly Bible study classes. Thus far there have been few complaints. He lives outside of Boston, Massachusetts.

Foreword

When you read "About the Author", Brian Marchionni describes his role in the church as one who "maintains the church web site, helps to lead weekly worship, and assists in teaching weekly Bible study classes." What he doesn't tell you is that he is also a most provocative and inspiring leader. No longer able to remain ignorant about the claims of Christianity himself, Brian is not prone to suffer lightly the myriad of reasons people give for rejecting those claims when they do so based solely on their choice to remain spiritually ignorant.

When it comes to the claims of Christ, some people are rightly turned off by Christians who give pat answers to serious questions. In *Permissive Ignorance*, watch out, because Brian not only refutes pat answers, he also refutes pat rejections with equal fervor. This isn't because he thinks he knows all the answers, but simply because he made the choice to intelligently consider some ideas he was never even open to hearing before. In doing so, his life was changed forever.

What I absolutely love about this book is the way Brian is able to confront the reader about such inconsistencies without being disrespectful or condescending. More than 700 years before Christ, God had some things He wished to say to the Kingdom of Judah while being held captive by the Babylonians. For this purpose He raised up the prophet Isaiah and began by saying, "Come now, let us reason together" (Isaiah 1:18).

Perhaps Brian Marchionni is just one of many such voices that God is using to raise the consciousness of people who are willingly being held captive by ignorance. As in the days of Isaiah, God has some things He wishes to say to this generation. *Permissive Ignorance* might just be another way of God saying, "Come now, let us reason together."

James M. Ennis
June 2002

Introduction

☙

Terminology

I would like to spend a few moments discussing a word that I will use throughout this book: Christianity. Today, the possible interpretations of this word seem limitless, so I think it is important to define what I mean by what has become such a broad term.

For the purposes of this book I intend Christianity to represent the belief system derived from the teachings of Jesus Christ as recorded in the Bible. Specifically:

- There is one, loving, eternal, all-powerful God who created the Universe and everything in it. God is Triune (one God in three distinct persons, *not* three gods): the Father, Son, and Holy Spirit.
- Jesus Christ is the second Person of the Trinity, and coequal with God the Father. Jesus became a man, and walked the earth as such, but was entirely without sin.
- Jesus was crucified, and died to pay the price for our sins against God.
- Jesus rose from the dead, and lives today in Heaven, the eternal home of God.
- By believing in Jesus, asking forgiveness for our sins, and making an effort to change our sinful ways (repent), we are *given* eternal life in Heaven with God. Salvation cannot be earned. Our faith in Jesus, and Jesus alone, is the deciding factor.
- The Holy Spirit is the third Person of the Trinity. He is not God the Father, or Jesus the Son, but a third distinct person who reproves, guides, comforts, and strengthens Christians.

- The sixty-six books of the Bible are the Word of God, and the ultimate basis for all Christian doctrine. The Bible is Truth.

I use the term "Christian" in this book as a means to describe a person as one who fundamentally believes in the statements above. My use of this word is intended to mean nothing more or less than the afore mentioned, I thus use it interchangeably with "believer."

BEHIND THE BOOK

In the interest of approachability, I have tried to minimize specific references to scripture in the pages that follow. Said omission notwithstanding, the Bible is the basis for all Christian dogma contained in this book.

There are literally hundreds of denominations of Christianity, and I have made every effort to avoid any discussion of them. The denominations exist almost entirely due to differences in emphasis or interpretation of certain parts of the Bible. None of the beliefs mentioned above fall into this realm of debate, however. I have consequently refrained from any discussion of these disputed issues, as I see no point in tripping over dollars to pick up pennies.

The questions and statements contained in this book are written to stimulate and edify the minds of its readers. They are not intended to judge or disparage anyone. Should any portion of this book come across as harsh, accusing, or judgmental, please rest assured that my directness is motivated solely from a desire to get people thinking. Some require a firmer push than others do, and consequently, stronger language. Were it possible to convey tone and body language via the written word, the text herein would be strictly sympathetic.

Finally, I would be remiss if I did not take at least

half a page to thank those that helped make this book possible. I would be equally remiss, however, if I devoted too much time describing the work in the kitchen to those simply wishing to get on with their meal. Thus, I will be brief, though let it say nothing of the depth of my gratitude.

I would like to thank my loving family. You are the loves of my life. No others on this earth do I hold closer to my heart; no others do I so admire.

To Barbara, Jim, Joey, Kathryn, Keith, Ravi, and all my brothers and sisters at Trolley Square: thank you for mountains of support, counsel, and warmth. I am a richer man having known each of you. Thank you also, Kate: your insight helped to shape this book; your companionship shaped this man.

Last, but far from least, I extend my deepest thanks to Randy, who took an interest in my soul years ago, and has since remained a dear friend and invaluable advisor.

When I told Randy that I wanted to write a book, he thought it was a great idea. When I told him that he was in it, he said, "Don't you want it to sell?"

Part I
❧
Motivation

"Men occasionally stumble over the truth, but most of them pick themselves up and hurry off as if nothing had happened."
-Sir Winston Churchill

ONE

☙

TESTIMONIAL NUMBER 19,948,342,644

"The Christian ideal has not been tried and found wanting. It has been found difficult, and left untried."
-G. K. Chesterton

THE GOOD SON

I was born into a Roman Catholic family in 1974. I was fortunate enough to be born into the care of two very special, loving parents. Looking back on my life, if I was allowed only one "thank you" to God for any of my earthly gifts, I would use it on my parents without batting an eye.

My parents grew up Catholic as well, and did their best to bring me up with similar values. My family and I would attend church every Sunday with what seemed to be our entire town. Like most children I didn't particularly care for church much more than I cared for any activity that required me to sit still and be quiet. At age eight, if I were ever given a choice between stillness and silence or motion and sound, I'd most certainly choose the latter. My preference aside, Sunday was for church and church was for Sunday. As I saw things, the requisite, post-church stop to Dunkin' Donuts was the only redeeming quality to Sunday morning.

16 - Permissive Ignorance

Despite my disdain for going to church, I did have a very strong belief in God the Father, Jesus His Son, and the Holy Spirit. I felt comfortable talking to Him with my problems, and knew I was right to believe in Him. A crucifix hung in my room, along with several prayer cards I had collected over the years. I even read a copy of the Children's Bible when I was eight.

Each night, after losing another battle in my ongoing war to stay up past my bedtime, my mother and father would tuck me into bed and write "Jesus" on my pillow with their finger. Once in bed, I would get back on my knees and say my prayers for the night. At one point my routine consisted of the Lord's Prayer, the Apostle's Creed, the Hail Mary, a recitation of the Ten Commandments, and a prayer for just about everybody in my life at the time. My fear was if I left anything out, something bad might happen.

"Sunday was for church and church was for Sunday."

It didn't take long for mom and dad to become concerned with the ever-increasing length of my prayer routine, and we soon spoke with a priest about my penchant for two-hour evening vigils. Looking back, my prayers only took about a half hour, all told. My wandering mind and subconscious crusade to stay up late stretched my prayers the extra hour and a half.

I went to CCE (Catholic Community Education) throughout elementary school and I received the sacraments up through Confirmation. It was Confirmation in eighth grade that marked the beginning of the end of my faith in God. Eighth grade also marked the first time I began to experiment with alcohol and tobacco; adolescence was ramping up at an alarming rate.

Within a year, I was no longer attending church with any regularity. I had become very active in my high school band and drama club, so there was little time for Jesus in my life. More obligations and responsibilities started to come my way, as well as more temptations. Since I had to make room for these, something had to go. Christianity was first on the list. I became too tired at night for prayers, and too old to be tucked in by my parents. My crucifix and prayer cards were slowly replaced with pictures of rock bands and other kitsch prevalent in the world of adolescent interior design.

Let's fast-forward eight years: as a senior in college at age twenty-two, my lifestyle was in stark contrast to anything I had ever learned through the church. Parties in college were frequent, and replete with every manner of intemperance and debauchery. I had all but utterly forsaken religion, *especially* Christianity.

I was bent on the fact that Christianity was a sad doctrine comprised of delusional-hypocrite-prudes who would bless themselves if they overheard somebody say "sex," lest their ears be soiled. I didn't want to be among legalistic fools too weak to face life without falling back on a fanciful collection of 2,000-year-old myths taken from a falsified book that served no practical purpose other than to create a series of draconian laws entirely inapplicable to my life.

> *"My lifestyle was in stark contrast to anything I had ever learned through the church."*

I was shocked at the atrocities committed in the history of Christianity. I believed the Bible to be utter nonsense: a collection of myths and legends manipulated by man for any number of reasons. I thought, deep down, all religions were the same: love one another, don't kill people, forgive others, and so on. I didn't need to be a part of any church. To my peers, and myself, I was a good

18 - Permissive Ignorance

person. Christianity just didn't make sense; it was quintessential nonsense. I could probably write another book just going over all the arguments I had against Christianity!

The transformation from the small boy saying his prayers each night to a young man who gladly denounced all things Christian took many years. Truth be told, I never even noticed the change. I'd have an interesting conversation with an atheist, hear a different spiritual view on life and death, or stumble upon a question about Christianity that I couldn't answer. Each day, the tide of the secular world would wash over me, slowly wearing away my faith, until there was little left. At the end of the day, what I clung to most was my own virtue: I was a good person.

> *"At the end of the day, what I clung to most was my own virtue."*

By society's standards, I *was* a good person, at least, on the outside. To most of the world, there really wasn't anything wrong with the way I was living my life. Almost all of my peers would have agreed. For many, it's a standard progression from youth to adulthood. Why did I consider myself a good person? I was polite, kempt, and respectful of authority. I did volunteer work, and never got into any trouble with the law. I was kind to others, and tried my best not to hurt people in any obvious way. Moreover, I never had any major conflicts with my family. Though my parents certainly would not have approved of my behavior, I never felt like I was rebelling against them to make up for an oppressive childhood. I was quite capable of having fun without succumbing to my darker vices.

I was working toward a degree in Computer Systems Engineering, which demanded tremendous amounts of time and effort. I never failed a class or

Testimonial Number 19,948,342,644 - 19

received an incomplete. I graduated with 142 credits in four years. I had accepted an excellent position as an electrical engineer for a Fortune-200 company seven months before I graduated. I graduated in excellent academic standing.

After graduation, I moved to upstate New York to begin my new job. In a matter of months, I was at the top of my game. While earning credit towards my master's degree, I excelled in all areas of my profession. I was given tremendous responsibilities and great raises. I was definitely on the fast track to move up the corporate ladder. The college-type party was still part of my life, but with much less frequency.

Through all this, my spiritual life did not die. I continued to pore over different philosophical and religious texts. Spiritism, astrology and even the religions of Native Americans intrigued me. Of all these, however, I was especially fond of the religions and philosophies of the Far East. I had immersed myself in Eastern thinking and religion, with Buddhism as my favorite.

"Christianity was still, without a doubt, a load of garbage."

Christianity was still, without doubt, a load of garbage entirely inapplicable to life in the 21st century.

My 25th year found me as I had always been: a very happy person. I had ups and downs, but such is life. I had a work hard-play hard attitude, unlimited potential in my career, a great bunch of friends, and a beautiful girlfriend. Little was missing from my life. I was a successful young professional.

I don't intend to sound boastful about my past. I simply want to relate to you my position before my rebirth into Christianity. Right now, many of you may be waiting for the tragedy; the horrible event I endured that would change me forever, and make me a Christian: the near-death experience, the dying family member, the miracle I witnessed, the dream I had, or my diagnosis of a terminal illness. Though I hate to disappoint, there is no story like that to tell.

THE GREAT RANDINO

In August of 1999, I moved to a new cube at work with my friend Randy. We two had met through work, and always enjoyed talking with each other. Randy was a senior engineer at my company, so he was a helpful teacher on a professional level as well as a good friend.

The day before I moved into my new cube, we were carrying on a casual conversation about our eating habits. I was a vegetarian at the time, and wouldn't eat any animal flesh (again, the Buddhism). Randy, a meat-eater, asked me, "Why do you think God put all the animals on the earth?" I responded with a grin, "That's an interesting question, because it assumes I believe that God put all the animals on the earth." Randy laughed, "Oh, we're going to have fun sitting together." We did.

Almost every day, Randy and I would walk down to the cafeteria and bring some lunch back to our cube. This was often the only chance we'd have during the day to unwind and talk. Since we were both engineers, our conversations often revolved around work, technology, or any number of other topics classically referred to as "geeky." As our friendship progressed, however, our conversations began to cover more personal topics: our past adventures, present struggles, and future dreams.

As time moved on, the topic of religion started to make its way into our lunchtime tête-à-tête. I would usually be the one to bring up the topic. I soon learned that Randy was a devout Christian. Though I believed Christianity to be nonsense at the time, I have always

Testimonial Number 19,948,342,644 - 21

practiced tolerance for other's values, and thus respected his belief. I told him how I was interested in Eastern thinking, and had gotten away from my Christian upbringing because it simply didn't make sense to me anymore. Buddhism, however, made sense to me in a way other religions hadn't, and seemed to unify so many of my morals and beliefs.

I should also mention that I thought it was *cool* to be interested in Buddhism. It seemed progressive, mysterious, and spiritual at once, like the type of doctrine that would make me the center of interesting conversations at parties. For the record, however, I didn't consider myself a Buddhist in the classical sense. During this time, I did not practice any religion at all. I preferred to think of myself as spiritual, instead of religious. Subconsciously, I believed that translated to "hip," instead of "square."

> *"I preferred to think of myself as spiritual, instead of religious."*

During the fall of that year, my workload at the office was reaching a record high, and my stress levels followed. On a particularly stressful day, I vented my frustration to Randy. Though I'm certain my question contained more expletives, I asked him something to the tune of, "How am I going to find balance in all of this mess?"

"I can tell you but you're not going to like the answer."

"How?"

"Christianity."

Though we both laughed, that day began a series of conversations that ultimately brought me back to Christ. In effect, I took Randy's bait. "Okay, Christianity, right? You buy all that bunk? Well, tell me

22 - Permissive Ignorance

this..." and so it went. Christianity was certainly never forced on me. Our conversations remained as pleasant and lively as ever, except now we were covering some heavy-duty territory. Through our discussions, for the first time in twenty-five years, I was beginning to understand what Christians believed, and more importantly, why and how. This was something my upbringing had never allowed me to ask. I was comfortable enough to ask Randy any question at all without fear of offending him.

Randy impressed me because none of my questions seemed to shake him in the least. Even when he didn't have an answer right away, he would simply say, "Hmm, good point. Let me check on that." Within a day or two, Randy would have an answer for me. No loose ends were ever left untied.

"By January of 2000, I was sold."

Eventually, I began to wonder how Randy, an analytical engineer like myself, was able to develop such faith, and how he was able to answer so many of my questions with such confidence. One day I asked, "Are there books on this sort of thing?" The next morning the answer lay on my chair. A small note read, "Give these books a try and let me know what you think."

The first books I read were those that addressed all of my tough questions about the existence of God, the validity of the Bible, and the Resurrection of Jesus. These books hit me hard, and chipped away at the fortress walls I had built up around my heart towards Christianity. As I began to see the abundance of historical, archeological, theological, and logical evidence for the deity of Christ, and the reasonableness of the Christian faith, it became harder and harder for me to find a valid reason to *dis*believe. The Christian faith was finally starting to make sense.

By January of 2000, I was sold. After countless hours of conversation with my friend, and hundreds of pages of text, I received Jesus Christ as my personal Lord and Savior, and gave my life over to Him. Once again, I became a Christian.

Some might remark on how my conversion bears a striking similarity to the way thousands are coaxed into joining various numbers of cults or sects. The key difference that I wish to point out is that Randy had nothing to gain by my acceptance of Christianity. He didn't try to get me to join or even go to his church. In fact, he never asked. My faith in Christ didn't permit him the collection of a membership fee, grant him some right to my services, or earn him salvation. He had no vested interest in me beyond our friendship.

"Every argument I ever put up slowly crumbled. I saw the Truth."

What's more, I cannot claim that I was any weaker or stronger than I had ever been. A busy period at work was certainly a catalyst, but my self-image, family life and body were all healthy and well. From the secular paradigm, I had nothing to gain by becoming Christian. At twenty-five, I wasn't exactly looking to subscribe to a doctrine that frowned upon heavy drinking, extra-marital sex, and dirty jokes, either.

I tell this story to illustrate the simple point that I've lived on both sides of the fence. I've been a believer and nonbeliever. As an intelligent, well-educated, strong-willed man, I was more than capable of arguing against the Christian religion. I dare say I was quite good at it. I wasn't searching for anything in my life more than anybody else. I was stable, successful, and happy, yet I converted. My whole case against Christianity, and every argument I ever put up, slowly crumbled. I saw the Truth.

I chose Jesus even though it meant I had to change the way I was living my life. My decision to embrace the Christian faith remains the best choice I have ever made and the most important thing I have ever done.

I half-jokingly titled this chapter "Testimonial Number 19,948,342,644." Though it would be impossible to count, I'm certain that this number approaches the right ballpark. Millions upon millions of people from millions of different backgrounds with millions of different stories to tell have arrived at the same point I did. I believe that to be remarkable in and of itself. Think of every possible vocation, background, generation, personality-type, or disposition, and I can guarantee you that men and women meeting whatever combination you can think of have come to Christ. Even more, their decision to do so changed their life.

Think about your story for a little while. Reflect on the changes that have taken place in your life. Think about your morals, ethics and philosophies. How did you get where you are today? Was Jesus ever part of your life? Where is He now? What has changed and why? Most likely your current beliefs have been a long time in the making, and continue to slowly evolve with time. Where do you think you're going?

I'll guess that you are open to more change since you are still reading this book. In fact, you're inviting change by reading it. Where do you think that motivation is coming from? What do you think you are searching for? Ruminate for a little while. I'll be asking you these questions again.

Two

☙

Strong Questions, Weak Answers

"A belief is not true because it is useful."
-Henri Frederic Amiel

Hello...Newton

Sir Isaac Newton, one of the foremost mathematicians and philosophers to ever have lived (and a Christian, by the way), was once quoted as saying, "To myself I seem to have been only a boy playing on the seashore, and diverting myself in now and then finding a smoother pebble or a prettier shell than ordinary, whilst the great ocean of truth lay all undiscovered before me."

Probably one of the largest fish in this unexplored ocean is manifested in the questions, "where did we come from?" and "where are we going?" Mankind has been focused on these questions throughout its history. Indubitably, they toe the line between science and religion. I would do these questions an injustice by even trying to estimate the countless volumes of books, experiments, theories, and conversations that have sought to answer them. Of these millions, however, relatively few have endured, and withstood the test of time. Many have faded into obscurity, been forgotten, or proven wrong.

What are your answers? Where do you think we came from? How did we get here? Some of you may answer, "Who cares? I'm more concerned with what's going on right now." Though I applaud your present-mindedness, recall that we do have a beginning and an end, even if we don't like to think about it. The natural world, so perfectly engineered, so breathtakingly beautiful, begs the question, "how did all this come about?" Hand in hand with the natural world is death. All living things die, thus demanding a very different, and even daunting question: "What happens *after* life?"

> *We seem to exert more effort planning our television-viewing schedule than planning our eternal destination.*

In my opinion, death seems to invoke much greater passion in today's world. It's a huge unknown for many. In a world where every living thing struggles constantly for the sake of self-preservation, the thought that there will come a day when we finally lose the battle is quite provocative. What next? I don't know about you, but I'd like to know where I'm going! Furthermore, I want to be prepared for it. Everybody hates to be the person who shows up at the costume party and forgot to dress up, right?

On some level, everybody wants to know the answers to these two questions. Very few seem to want to do the work to get there. We seem to exert more effort planning our television-viewing schedule than planning our eternal destination. A quick, easy, gloss-over of an answer seems to be enough to satisfy most.

Pushing such thoughts out of our minds effectively buries our heads in the sands of ignorance: just don't think about it, and hope for the best. For some, this is a defense mechanism when it comes to thoughts that may be unpleasant. This attitude reminds me of a woman I knew who began to develop a lump on her neck, yet refused to visit a doctor for fear she might find out she had cancer. Are you afraid to find out about Christianity for fear it might be true? Fear not, the Truth of Christianity is far removed from anything I would consider unpleasant.

What is "the best" anyway? Is it some sort of afterlife? Many non-Christians seem to think that if there really is a God, they can plead ignorance to Him, and nothing bad will happen to them after death. This falls into what I like to call the "happy grandpa" image of God:

"Are you afraid to find out about Christianity for fear it might be true?"

We find God on a rocking chair in Heaven, with a long white beard, which he gently strokes as wisps of smoke from his pipe encircle his head. "Well, boys will be boys, I guess!" he says, as people live their life any way they see fit. When judgment comes, a quick, "Oh, sorry, God, I didn't know all this stuff was real!" will be enough to get any decent person through the pearly gates.

Aside from the fact that this isn't the way God is, or how He works, I would say that it's going to be a hard sell to try to convince Him you didn't know He was real if you never put forth any sincere effort to find out about Him.

How much thinking have you done about these types of questions? What do you think will happen to you when you die? What questions do you have about how life began, or how it will end? What sort of work have you done to answer those questions?

DENIAL ISN'T JUST A RIVER IN EGYPT

Most know that Christianity claims to have the answers to the tough, eternal questions we have in life.

28 - Permissive Ignorance

The problem is that too many don't like them, because they are more than answers. Christian answers are not always easy to accept or understand. Furthermore, they often demand a change in your attitude or lifestyle.

Christianity doesn't always provide easy answers. To this end, many people look to find a few holes or inconsistencies that they can't understand or accept about Christianity, and then throw in the towel. "Sorry, I don't believe Jesus really rose from the dead." The end. "I saw a guy with rimmed glasses and a tweed jacket say on TV that Jesus was a myth. There were lots of books behind him, so he seemed to know what he was talking about." Case closed.

This sort of attitude is characteristic of a person who really isn't all that committed to learning about Christianity in the first place. They had their answer of "no" loaded a long time ago; they just needed a reason to pull the trigger. Is that the type of person you are? Do you just abandon what you're doing the moment you stumble? Do you stop searching the minute you can't find an answer? I sure hope not. People who portray such an attitude are, for lack of a gentler term, quitters.

"Every skill that you have is the product of your own tenacity."

Every skill that you have is the product of your own tenacity. Could you speak perfectly when you first tried? No. But you kept trying didn't you? How about learning to walk and run? Playing an instrument? Beating a record in sports? Grasping a difficult concept in school? Finishing a tedious book?

In countless examples throughout your life, you've been stumped: you couldn't answer a question, you couldn't finish the race, or you didn't know what to do. The key is that you kept trying. You didn't give up.

Whatever you were pursuing was important enough for you to pick yourself up off the ground and try again. As the old adage goes, "It doesn't matter if you get knocked down. The important thing is what you do next." I couldn't agree more.

Quitting happens when we don't care enough about what we're doing. In other words, the price outweighs the reward. I've been a drummer for over nineteen years. Many times, I get angry with myself, and my lack of ability, or listening to a more accomplished drummer play humbles me. Though this may be discouraging at times, I would never quit. I keep trying to improve because drumming is important to me. I love to make music, and it is a very special part of my life. The difficulty of practicing a certain rhythm or pattern over and over again isn't as important to me as the benefit of becoming a better player.

"Quitting happens when we don't care enough about what we're doing."

So, if you have a few issues with Christianity, and *aren't putting forth any effort* to resolve them, you're making a bold statement. You're not saying "I don't believe in Christianity because I don't believe X, Y, and Z." You're saying, "I don't *want* to believe in Christianity. It's not important to me." You see the difficulties of justifying the Christian religion, or living the Christian life as being greater than the benefits.

PERMISSIVE IGNORANCE

I entitled this book *Permissive Ignorance* because I feel it best describes the condition of most who reject Christianity. Before I became Christian, I had any number of reasons for keeping from the faith. Each of these was due to my own ignorance about the very faith I was rejecting, and the numerous historical, logical, scientific, and theological arguments that assert its validity. As I discovered, deep down, I was *choosing* to remain ignorant of Christianity.

In today's world, I feel that ignorance is almost always the result of a personal choice. For instance, I am ignorant of the Gaelic language, and cannot speak a word. This is entirely by my own choosing. Had I the desire to learn however, I could certainly do so through any number of books, videos, or classes. My ignorance is a choice.

Granted, it is far from practical to remove any trace of ignorance from our lives. In languages alone I could devote a lifetime to study, but I would still die ignorant of hundreds. Indeed, we must choose, and carefully, that of which we are to remain ignorant. I fervently believe the doctrine of Christianity as presented in the Bible is too compelling, too bold, and too important to ignore.

"I was choosing to remain ignorant of Christianity."

The Christian faith is very reasonable. It isn't all smoke, mirrors, and "blind faith," as many prefer to think. (Actually, if you think about the word "faith" for a little while longer, you may find that "blind faith" is somewhat redundant.) It isn't a collection of myths that have been manipulated and tainted by man. A doctrine that has been despoiled by man is not a part of Biblical Christianity anyway, but rather, a derivative. All the evidence to support these claims is out there.

There is a sound rebuttal to every single hole one might try to poke in the fabric of the Christian faith. The problem is that too few people actually do the legwork required to reach this conclusion. This is permissive ignorance. Too few do the research.

Furthermore, I believe that God wants us to do the research. The Bible tells us to love Him with all our heart, soul, strength, and *mind*. Nobody can deny that we have a remarkable piece of machinery locked up in our skulls. Certainly, it is there for a reason beyond eating and breathing. God gave us a wonderful capacity for thought and analysis; I'm sure we were meant to use it.

What's more, God knows that Christianity can stand up to the closest scrutiny. Christianity does not demand belief in the illogical, nor does it require faith without reason. Faith is essential, yes, but Christianity is meant to be everything: your heart, soul, strength, and mind, all the major components that make up who you are. Also, don't forget that faith is required to *dis*believe in God as well.

"God wants us to do the research."

WAY BETTER THAN YOUR 401(K)

We've just established an important fact: you quit something when the difficulties outweigh the benefits. So if you've "quit" or rejected Christianity, you don't see the benefits as all that beneficial. So, what is the benefit to Christianity? What will belief in Jesus bring you? Let us begin with one of our big questions.

What is going to happen to you when you die? Would you like to know? As I mentioned earlier, most of the world, America in particular, seems terrified of death. Death is something we don't like to talk or even think about. We worship youth and beauty. Aging and dying rank among our biggest fears. Guess what? It's coming. You have a finite amount of time left here on the earth, and you are powerless to change the simple fact that you will die.

I don't mean to be morbid. For sure, dwelling on

our mortality is equally as dangerous as ignoring it. However, remaining cognizant of the fact that our time on earth is limited is something far too many people are able to shrug off for far too long.

One of the biggest benefits Christianity can claim is eternal life in Heaven with God. As a believer in Jesus Christ, you can face death and know where you are going. You can lay on your deathbed in peace. You don't have to worry about a thing. Furthermore, you can know that you're going to be spending eternity in the best place ever: Heaven! How could you do better than that?

The joy in Heaven is unparalleled to anything we could imagine on earth. My words couldn't possibly describe it. No suffering, no pain, no problems. Take a moment and think of the happiest you've ever been. What is your most cherished and pleasant memory? Take that, and multiply it by the number of atoms in the sun. Now you might be getting close to the magnitude of joy you'll experience in Heaven. The Bible is very clear about the fact that God's gift of salvation to us will bring about unfathomable joy.

"How confident do you feel right now in facing death?"

How confident do you feel right now in facing death? Realize, of course, that you may face it much sooner than you think. I don't mean to be gruesome, but nobody can predict the future. Many will continue to put off their thoughts of their death, or even their investigation of Christianity, thinking that they have time. The unpleasant fact of the matter is they don't *know* they have time. None of us know when or how we will die; putting off your thoughts on mortality or your research into Christianity to another day is risky business. Remember, you only get one chance at life.

What do you hang your hat on? Is death just the

end? Do we lose consciousness, and that's it? Are we just chemicals? Is there more to us than just carbon, hydrogen, and oxygen? Do we have a spirit? What do you think happens to that spirit, or soul, when we die?

Whatever you think, you'd better be sure. If you aren't, you are taking a tremendous gamble. Eternity is an awfully long time, and it's even longer than that. Imagine emptying all the contents of the world's oceans with an eyedropper. That's a blink of an eye to eternity. Imagine walking to the nearest star. That's gravy to eternity. Where would you like to spend all of that time? There are two options: Heaven and Hell. The former is much more pleasant than the latter. Everything that Heaven is, Hell isn't, and it lasts forever.

So there's your first benefit: eternal life in Heaven versus eternal life in Hell. You get to spend eternity in the most joyous place imaginable. Not bad. In fact, I can't think of anything better. I can't think of any amount of suffering or pain I could endure here for my brief time on earth that *wouldn't* be worth eternal life in Heaven.

> *"Eternity is an awfully long time."*

If you like arithmetic, here is a problem: determine the percentage of your existence that will be spent on earth. Mathematically speaking, the correct answer is precisely 0%. Most will live for about 80 years on earth, then spend eternity either in Heaven or Hell. 80 years divided by infinity is 0, giving a whopping 0%.

I DOUBLE DARE YOU

Consider the following scenario: you and I are standing by Niagara Falls. I have placed before you ten different capsules, one of which you are to ride over the falls. Attached to each capsule is a twenty-page summary written by the engineers who designed it.

34 - Permissive Ignorance

In each, they give a list of their credentials, previous trial runs over the falls, and why they think their capsule is the best.

I tell you that in exactly four hours, I am going to force you to choose a capsule and ride it over the falls. Refusal to choose isn't an option. I inform you that only one of the capsules will carry you over safely. All the others will result in a rather unpleasant death. I also explain that the answer to which capsule is the safe one is readily apparent after reading the engineer's summaries for each.

I give you a pat on the back, set my stopwatch to count down the four hours, and leave. For a moment, you stand and look over the ten capsules. Some are ratty looking on the outside, but seem very stable. Others are very fancy, with a slick outer shell, and plush interior. You have four hours, and your life hangs in the balance. What would you do next?

"Why take such a huge risk?"

Unless you have a fondness for taking meaningless and severe chances with your life, I would hope that you'd spend the next four hours reading the engineer's summaries. Why would you do that? Because the stakes are high! If you choose wrong, you're going to die a horrendous death.

The stakes are even higher when you consider your death here on earth. Why do so many people refrain from reading the engineer's summaries then? Why take such a huge risk? It can be confusing, for sure. There are much more than just ten "summaries" to read out there. There are thousands. You are welcome to read up on all of them, though I strongly recommend you read about Christianity first. It's the only capsule that will get you over the falls safely. You can take my word for it, or you can find out for yourself. I guarantee you'll arrive at the same conclusion I did. You should probably do *something* though. The stakes are high, and the clock is running.

HELL, NO?

Now, imagine that you are dying. Slowly, you feel your life slip away, and you breathe your last breath. An instant later, you are faced with God. In a moment you realize that you were wrong to reject Christ. Now, it's too late. Think of the despair, as you come to the realization that you lived your whole life with the opportunity for salvation, but chose to deny it. Think of the hopelessness you would feel knowing that there is no changing things now. For eternity, you will be in Hell. All of this is because you decided not to accept God's gift to you. You were too busy to explore Christianity a little bit more. Life kept getting in the way.

> "In a moment you realize that you were wrong to reject Christ."

You didn't want to live your life by anybody's rules but your own. Now, you live with the consequences of your decision forever. There is no reprieve, and no possibility for change. You are utterly, eternally, and hopelessly lost.

It is a hard fact to face. Many people escape it with further denial, "If God is truly loving, how could He allow that, then? If He loves me, why would He send me to Hell? Why do such a horrible thing to me? I'm a good person, right? Why wouldn't He let me know that He was real while I still had the chance to change?"

The doctrine of Hell has certainly turned many would-be Christians away because it is hard to reconcile the punishment of Hell with the love of God. Shifting the paradigm to God's viewpoint, however, helps to answer part of the question: God won't send you to Hell, you'll send yourself.

36 - Permissive Ignorance

You had a choice all of your life: Jesus, or not Jesus. Each day of your life, you had a choice between the two, and you consistently chose to deny Jesus. You didn't believe in God. You didn't believe in Jesus. You ignored His word. God is giving you what you asked for. You've said, throughout your life, "I don't want God. I don't want to find out about Him, or follow Him." God says, "okay." Separation from God is Hell. You asked for Hell, so God is giving it to you.

I am invariably asked by friends at this point about the man or woman who has never heard of Jesus, or the aboriginal tribe that has rarely had contact with the outside world, and thus does not know the Bible more than any other book. What of them? Are they damned? Frankly, I don't know. I do know, however, that God is loving, righteous, and just. I therefore have supreme confidence in His ability to deal with such men and women after death.[1]

God knows that souls will suffer in Hell, and He doesn't want that for anybody. He loves us, remember, but we have to want to be with Him, too. He paid the ultimate price so we could avoid damnation, but we have to accept His gift of salvation for the transaction to be complete. As the expression goes, "you can lead a horse to water, but you can't make him drink." God didn't create robots. We all have free will, and thus the choice to follow Him or not.

"You had a choice all your life: Jesus or not Jesus."

Imagine that you walk to work everyday, up hill, both ways, through six feet of snow (like my grandfather used to do). One day, I call you up and tell you that

---

[1] The concern for people who have never heard of Jesus is likely a key motivator for those who have traveled to all different parts of the globe and preached the Gospel as Christian missionaries.

because I'm such a nice guy, I will give you a new 4X4 truck to drive to work every day. All you have to do is drop by my place, pick up the keys, and drive. You have a choice: pick up the keys and drive to work, or continue to walk each day.

As a nice guy, I don't want you to walk to work every day, but I can't force you to accept my gift. You have to come over and accept my generosity. That's how it works. God has offered us eternal salvation in Heaven through His son, Jesus. It's a gift. We don't deserve it, and we can't earn it. All we can do is accept it, and try to change.

Notice in the above analogy that for you to truly accept my gift of the truck, you must use it. You could easily take the truck, leave it parked in your driveway, and still walk to work each day. Changing your routine to use the truck each day constitutes true acceptance of my gift to you, and my true intentions in giving it. In the same way, truly accepting God's gift to us involves our effort to change, and repent from sin. If you do believe in God, and understand that your salvation is contingent on His mercy to you through Jesus, repentance will follow naturally, as you choose to behave in a manner more pleasing to God.

> *"God has revealed Himself to you many times in many miraculous ways."*

"Why won't God perform a miracle for me, so I will believe? If He has the power to do anything, surely He could appear to me one day, and perform some supernatural act so I will know that He is God." The answer to this question is that He already has, thousands of times. God has revealed Himself to you many times, in many miraculous ways.

Consider the world we live in. It had to be created

at some point, by something. If you think science has that question neatly wrapped up, I hope I don't shatter your world by saying that you're wrong. There are as many unanswered questions and inconsistencies in what science can tell us about our origin as there are stars in the sky. Even the most skeptic, non-Christian scientist in the world will tell you that science isn't even close to having our origins explained away.

What about the amazing stories and testimonies you hear from others? Are they all crazy? If so, that sure makes for a lot of hallucinating delusionals out there. Consider all of the people in the world that have faced (and face) execution, torture and excommunication for the sake of their belief in Jesus. This was especially prevalent in the early days of Christianity.

What of the miracle recoveries we've all heard about? What about the miracle of life itself? What about all the "coincidences" that have happened in your life and the lives of others? What's it going to take? How many "coincidences" do you have to see, experience, or hear about to believe that God is running the show? Do you want a personal appearance by God to tell you what to do? Should He tell you that He is real and you need to believe in Him? He's done that. His name was—is—Jesus.

The truth is that you've hardened your heart. You've chosen to explain away all of God's work by other means. If God visibly appeared to you right now, said, "I'm real. Believe in me," and then vanished, would that be enough? Or, would you explain it away as something weird that happened to you: a dream, a hallucination, or a practical joke? What if tomorrow night, the world was flooded with the breaking news that a group of scientists has unequivocally proven the existence of God and Truth of the Bible? What if for weeks the newspapers were just overflowing with this story, and all scientific institutions agreed? Would you explain this away? Would you find another reason for rejecting God, or would your skepticism simply vanish? What would it take? How many times does God need to show you that He's real? We should only need to be told once. Instead, God tells us every second of the day. Are you listening? Be still for a moment and listen: He's telling you again, right now.

God is giving you another chance through this book. Right now, as you read, you're presented again with an opportunity to accept Jesus. You can't plead ignorance when you're judged. When you are faced with God, do you think you'll be able to fool Him? God knows your heart and mind better than you do. Do you think you can convince Him that you just never had the time to find out about Christ while you were alive? That you were too busy? That you really didn't know?

"How many times does God need to show you that He's real?"

God has revealed Himself to you again and again. This book is yet another indication that you should look into Christianity some more. What are you going to do? Will you wave your hands in the air and shrug this off? Are you going to put this book down, and live the rest of your life in denial of God and Jesus? Are you going to take that risk?

Three

❦

Mythinformation

"The great enemy of truth is very often not the lie - deliberate, contrived, and dishonest - but the myth - persistent, persuasive and realistic."
-John F. Kennedy

Lame-o-rama

A myth is a fictitious person, place or happening. I would expand this definition to include misconceptions about people and beliefs. Our culture today has developed a wide range of myths about the Christian religion as another means of "disproving" and rejecting it.

Along with myths, our world has also developed very strong stereotypes about Christians. There is certainly a stigma associated with being a Christian in today's culture. These stereotypes, prejudices, and myths all work together to keep us away from doing the research. We don't *want* to become Christians. If we do, we'll become "one of those people." Perhaps worst of all, we might become unpopular.

Allow me to illustrate with this watered down version of what I might have said about Christians a few years ago:

Christians are lame! *They have no fun at all. They walk through life denying themselves almost every pleasure on earth. They are oversensitive prudes with little or no sense of humor. They have no sense of fashion, listen to lame music, and watch lame TV shows. They sit at home reading the Bible all day before going to bed...at 8:00 p.m.*

Why would I want to be a Christian? Why would I want to take away all that I enjoy in life? I want to be happy, not miserable as all the Christians seem to be. Why should I be a self-righteous killjoy?

Have you ever found yourself thinking similar thoughts? What stereotypes do you have about Christians? If you were to write down the first few things that come to mind when somebody says the word "Christian," or "Jesus," what would you write? What thoughts do these words provoke? How well founded do you think they are?

In a society of increasing diversity and awareness, few would argue that harboring any stereotype or prejudice is deplorable. We've all seen the horrors that stereotypes and prejudice have wrought on our society. Today hundreds of companies, universities, and organizations work hard to help counteract such destructive thoughts.

"Prejudices and stereotypes thrive on misinformation."

For sure, prejudices and stereotypes thrive on misinformation. The more ignorant you are about a certain culture or concept, the more likely you will harbor a prejudice or stereotype. They will typically work into our thoughts through casual observations regarding outward appearances, and information that we take out of context. Even more common, prejudices develop when we witness a subset of a certain group of people behaving in a particular way, then automatically—and erroneously—assume all others of said group are the same.

A while back, a friend and I were arguing about state police troopers. To put it lightly, he hated all state troopers. He saw all of them as power-hungry, hateful, egomaniacs out for nobody but themselves. He based this information on the fact that every time he saw state troopers, they looked mean and threatening. He also had two personal experiences that he drew from to feed his prejudice.

What do you think? Are all state troopers power-hungry, hateful, egomaniacs? Of course not! That's a horrendous generalization. I'm certain that there are some state troopers who fit this description, but I bet there are accountants, musicians, cashiers, politicians, doctors, and engineers who fit the bill too.

Now, I won't pretend to know why the state troopers my friend had seen always looked so mean and threatening. Maybe it is part of a state trooper's job to behave that way. After all, their goal is to keep the peace, and fight crime. Perhaps they try to look scary and intimidating so people will think twice before breaking the law. Perhaps they portray that attitude as a simple means of quelling criminal intentions: they want their interactions with you to be unpleasant. If getting a speeding ticket involved a pleasant conversation with a slap on the wrist, I probably wouldn't worry about breaking the speed limit.

Which one of us is right? If my friend and I wanted to know for sure, we would have to look into it a little bit. I could interview some policemen, and ask about their training. I'm sure there are plenty of books that speak about the subject, too. It isn't fair for us to assume to know the truth given our limited knowledge of their situation.

44 - Permissive Ignorance

Are you allowing prejudices and stereotypes to grow within you? Maybe you've met a few Christians that fit the description I gave earlier in the chapter. Does that mean that all Christians are like that? Does it mean that you will have to be like that if you become a Christian? Are all Christians self-righteous, Bible-thumping prudes? Are all of them confrontational about their faith, constantly pushing you and others to change your sinful ways? Do you think that is what the Bible teaches? Self-righteousness? Judgment of others? Hatred? Oppression? It might be worth finding out for yourself.

Think back over your life to all of the times you had an opinion about something before you became truly familiar with it. For example, maybe you saw a preview to a movie once and were certain that it wasn't worth seeing. Maybe after meeting a co-worker you immediately thought they were going to be a real bear to work with. How many times have you had such thoughts and months later realized that you were completely wrong? I can't even begin to count the number of times I've been wrong about somebody I've met. "She's really quiet." "He's too pushy." "She seems selfish." "He doesn't seem too confident in himself." The list goes on to include movies I've seen, events I've attended, and foods I've eaten.

"Are all Christians self-righteous, Bible-thumping prudes?"

The bottom line is that none of us have any business evaluating something in ignorance. If you've made the decision that Christianity is for the birds, or at least, not for you, ask yourself, "how much do I really know about Christianity?" Are your arguments based upon a solid foundation of knowledge and understanding? Or are they based upon an assortment of rumors, personal observations, and stories you've heard?

CROSS EXAMINATION

Pretend you have been charged with rejecting Christianity, and must defend yourself before a grand jury. The prosecution wishes to prove that you are not making an informed decision. What is your defense? Consider the following arguments and rebuttals, some of which are taken from actual conversations I've had with friends.

"It just doesn't make any sense to me that there could be a loving God who allows so many to suffer."

Great question! How much have you done to make sense of that? What books have you read that attempt to answer your question? No doubt, it's probably the most common question non-Christians ask (actually, Christians, too). There are many books that deal with this very topic in detail, providing satisfying answers. Have you read any? Do you think suffering would exist in the world if sin did not? Whose fault is suffering, really? God's or ours? Millions die of hunger each year. If merely 5% of the food America *throws away* each day were recovered, 4 million more people could be fed.[2] Do you think there is enough food to go around in the world? Are wars God's fault? Are murder, rape, and torture? Environmental destruction? Would cancer and other diseases remain prevalent in a world free of toxicity, promiscuity, or carelessness? Next time you blame God for suffering, take a good hard look at the human race and our history of sin. As Oswald Chambers said, "In our

"Whose fault is suffering, really?"

---

[2] U.S. Environmental Protection Agency, *Waste Not Want Not: Feeding the Hungry and Reducing Solid Waste through Food Recovery*, 1997, p.11.

mental outlook we have to reconcile ourselves to the fact of sin as...the explanation of the grief and sorrow in life."[3]

"When I was in college there was a group of Christian activists who were judgmental and cruel to other non-Christians."

It is indeed very sad when people use their faith to justify acts of hatred. I deal with this issue specifically in chapter 4. What does this have to do with the Christian faith, though? If the Surgeon General were a smoker, would that make the warnings on packs of cigarettes lies? Does hypocrisy affect truth? Another thing to ask yourself is if you are rejecting Christ, or the judgmental Christian activists. Rejecting the activists doesn't need to affect your view of Christ.

"Christianity (or the existence of God) can't be scientifically proven."

This is a big hang-up for many. The most common pitfall here is that people are mixing apples and oranges. Many people don't understand what it means for something to be scientifically proven. For example, "scientifically prove" love for me. Can you do it? No way. Yet, love exists, does it not? How do you know? Because you can find a million other people who agree with you? Christianity can claim that too. Maybe you believe love exists because psychologists and other scientists write textbooks about love. Christians have plenty of scientists, too (and textbooks). Do you believe that love exists because you've felt it? Funny, that's one of the ways—and there are many—that we know God exists: we feel Him. Even if I were to ignore the above argument, can you scientifically *disprove* God's existence?

---

[3] Oswald Chambers, *My Utmost for His Highest*, (Uhrichsville, OH: Barbour, 1963).

"I don't believe in creationism."

Do you also realize that evolution isn't proven either? It's a theory, right along with the Big Bang. In fact, much of these theories require great faith! Yet, most people tend to find evolution more believable. Why? Because that's what you learned in school? (Just a reminder, if you went to a public school, they usually won't teach anything else due to the separation of church and state.) Do you believe because hundreds of scientists have written books about it? Because people with PhD's endorse it? Because it's mentioned on the Discovery Channel? The Christian faith can boast the same on all accounts. How many books have you read which seek to refute evolution? If your answer is "none," then you've really only heard one side of the story, haven't you?

I should mention here that belief in creationism isn't necessarily essential to salvation through Jesus. Nor does the biblical account of creation necessarily contradict evolution. Many Christians are believers of evolution. It is doubtful that we will know the specifics of our creation during this life. Don't let this keep you from Jesus. It is not as important.

"I don't believe in the Bible."

This statement presupposes that you've *read* the Bible. Have you? Many people I meet disagree with the Bible but have never actually read it. Usually, they know only a few verses or principles. They usually take these out of context, and miss their true meaning. Why? Because they've never read the whole thing, or even a significant part of it. If you want to claim disagreement with something you should understand it first. Do you understand the Bible?

"I don't believe the Bible is accurate."
    Again, let me ask, what evidence do you have to support your belief? Have you ever read about how Christians claim to know the Bible is the true Word of God? Have you ever considered it peculiar how quickly you will believe what you read in newspapers, magazines, e-mails, or other popular books? Why not believe a book that has withstood thousands and thousands of years of time, oppression and intense (sometimes even unjust) scrutiny?

    The list can go on and on. If you try, you may find that you don't have as many solid answers as you once thought. You may realize that many of your arguments aren't as well founded as you might like to think. I certainly did.

HEAVEN ON EARTH?
    In the previous chapter, I touched upon a major benefit of believing in Jesus Christ: eternal life with God in Heaven. In actuality, there are many more. Christian life isn't one of misery and denial. It is positively wonderful, and amazingly rewarding. It fulfills the very fiber of our being, and gives us a great sense of purpose and peace. Unfortunately, to truly do it justice, it must be experienced. As a Christian, God will bless you in this life as well as the next.
    Please don't get me wrong, though. The Christian life isn't easy. Your problems won't just melt away the moment you believe in Jesus. Like everything in life though, the more you put in, the more you get out. It's a simple fact of existence. I think a sign outside of a church summed it up best: "The work is hard, the hours are long...but the retirement benefits are out of this world."

I should take this opportunity to make an important point: one must be careful not to get too wrapped up in what God can do for them. It is fantastic to think of the glory of life in Heaven, as well as the blessings He will bestow upon you while on earth. Too much concentration on these things, however, will actually lead you away from God. We should love God because of who He is, not because of what He can do for us. I think this is a major reason why many backslide: they will come to Christ and live a Christian life for a while, but at the first sign of hardship, they will back away.

> *"We should love God for who He is, not because of what He can do for us."*

The Christian experience is truly amazing in every sense of the word, but it is important not to let yourself be deceived: it is not all roses. Any mature Christian will tell you, though, it's worth it! Even ignoring the amazing and incomprehensible reward of Heaven, it's worth it.

MYOPIA AND YOUROPIA

If there is one trait that most human beings share, it's impatience. Generally speaking, most of us want things right *now*. We are always asking ourselves, "What's easier for me *now*? What will bring me more pleasure *now*?" We don't like to think ahead. Our capacity for critical thinking, and our ability to perceive the consequences of our actions is often overshadowed by our lack of patience.

At the writing of this book, compact fluorescent light bulbs cost almost 20 times more than conventional incandescent bulbs, but they last about 10 times longer, and use about 75% less power. Over the life span of the light bulb, purchasing a compact fluorescent can save you upwards of $45 in electrical bills.[4] Why are incandescent bulbs still more common in households? I'm sure there are many reasons, but primarily, it's because we want our extra money *now*. If I'm in a store, and I see a $1 incandescent light bulb right next to a $20 compact florescent, without thinking, I see 19 reasons why I should get the cheaper bulb.

The compact fluorescent light bulb is perhaps an extreme example, still it underscores the fact that so much of what our society works for, and pays for, is instant gratification. We pay huge mark-ups on items if we can get them faster. Indeed, if we were to boil down our objectives as a race over the past few centuries, the main theme would come down to the word "faster." So much of what we work for as a world is speed. Think of all the technological innovations that have taken place over the past hundred years. So many of them revolve around the simple concept of getting things done faster.

There is something to be said for efficiency and convenience, for sure. Expeditious thinking is not all bad in certain areas of life. When it comes to matters of personal development, though, speed is not the answer. No natural process wants to be hurried. In fact, no natural process *is* hurried without something else paying the price. We don't just become mature adults when we turn eighteen. It's impossible. Maturity takes years upon years to develop, and there is no way to make somebody grow up faster.

> "When it comes to matters of personal development, speed is not the answer."

I believe this penchant for speed combined with our bent towards shortsightedness work hand in hand in

---

[4] Howard Geller, *Compact Fluorescent Lighting*, http://www.aceee.org/press/op-eds/op-ed1.htm.

keeping us from Christianity. The ways of sin, or the way of the world, is often the quicker, easier path. The Christian life focuses on things like patience and perseverance. These two things aren't very popular in the 21st century. Even more, researching Christianity takes some time and effort. The Bible won't read itself, after all! Consistent with this, your questions or doubts about the Christian faith will remain unanswered unless you take action to resolve them.

"I'll worry about God when I'm ready to die." "I'm busy right now; Jesus can wait." Is your shortsightedness keeping you from God? Remember how short life is here on earth. Based upon an eternal scale, our earthly lives begin and end in less than a blink of an eye. If you are only concerned about the next day, month, or year, you are doing yourself an injustice. I agree that one cannot dwell on the future, but just as well, it cannot be ignored.

"Will worldly things matter to you when you are faced with death?"

Thinking only of what will become of you in this life on earth is dangerous. There is an infinitely larger portion of your life to be lived on the other side of eternity. Do you know where that will be?

Remember also that procrastination, shortsightedness, or taking the quicker, easier way through life always has a price. Consider the price of living your life apart from God. Will worldly things matter to you when you are faced with death? How strongly will you oppose God on your deathbed? Will you argue against Christianity with the same vigor? How unshakable are your present beliefs?

MISSION: IMPOSSIBLE

Some people use their past as a means of avoiding

commitment to Christ. Their assumption is that since they've already lived such a sinful life, it is too late for them to be saved. This argument bears a striking similarity to one given by chronic cigarette smokers. "I've been smoking for ten years, quitting now won't do me any good." All such arguments, of course, are flimsy at best. In the same way that it is never too late to quit smoking, it is never too late to turn your life over to Christ.

No matter what your past, God will forgive you. This is one of the most central themes in the Bible. Your sins may be forgiven, once and for all, as if you had never sinned at all. All you have to do is ask, and change your ways. It doesn't matter how long you've sinned, how badly you've sinned, or how often you've sinned.

"In essence, Christians are Christians because of sin."

God will forgive you. The Bible is absolutely abounding with every manner of example, teaching, and message that God loves us, and will forgive us of our sins through our faith in Jesus.

A popular myth today is the assumption that one must be "good enough" to be a Christian, or will never have what it takes to make it into Heaven. The misconception is that a Christian must live a perfect life, free from sin. Wrong again! Christian people sin too, and don't let anybody tell you otherwise. In essence, Christians are Christians because of sin. If I was without sin, I would not need to be Christian. We are all human, and it is our nature to sin. We cannot possibly live to the standard set by Jesus, which is why we need Him for forgiveness of our sins, and for help to repent.

Being a Christian means that your attitude towards sin changes. You recognize your need for forgiveness, and make an effort to change your ways. You no longer *practice* sin. There is a popular Christian bumper sticker that says it well: "Christians aren't perfect, just forgiven."

Don't reject Christianity because you feel it is too hard for you. Find out about it first. God doesn't expect us to be perfect over night. In fact, we are perfect only through Christ. Like everything else in life, it takes time and practice to mature. Most of us weren't handed a textbook of advanced mathematics in first grade. It takes years of study and practice to reach that level. Start with the basics of Christianity, and work your way up. God will be there with you every step of the way.

When you accept Jesus as your savior and invite Him into your life, He will begin to change you from the inside out on a day-by-day basis. A popular misconception is that in becoming Christian, we have to do all the work ourselves. Quite to the contrary, it is God who does the work! God will change you in an amazing way. C.S. Lewis summed it up beautifully in his book, *Mere Christianity*, by saying that Christians do not believe God loves us because we are righteous, but rather that God will make us righteous because He loves us.[5]

"Start with the basics of Christianity and work your way up."

Those who look at Christianity and say, "You can't do this, or you can't do that" don't realize that through Jesus, you eventually won't want to do "this," or won't want to do "that." The "don't do's" that keep a lot of people away from Christianity, eventually become "I don't care to's" as Jesus starts changing their hearts. New Christians need to establish a relationship with Jesus, and not worry about the "don't do's." Jesus will take care of the "don't do's" in your life when you are ready to

---

[5] C.S. Lewis, *Mere Christianity*, (New York, NY: Touchstone, 1996).

handle the change.

This isn't to say that all temptation will quickly melt away. You will still be temped, but your attitude will change to sin, and ultimately your actions will follow. Remember that temptation isn't sin. You must act upon temptation for it to become sin.

As a follower of Jesus, you will find that the "difficult" choices you face in your life between sin and God will become easier with time. In his book, *How to Say No to a Stubborn Habit*, Erwin Lutzer likens us to a beam of steel directly in the center of two magnets: one representing God, or righteousness, and the other representing the world, or sin. At first, both magnets pull on the steel with equal strength, but if the beam moves slightly towards one of the magnets, the pull of the other will be weakened. In addition, the pull of the first magnet will become stronger, and harder to break.[6]

> *"The longer you lean in one direction, the stronger the attraction will be to remain where you are."*

This illustration can represent any set of choices in life. You'll find that the longer you lean in one direction, the stronger the attraction will be to remain where you are. Christian life is no different. It will take effort to dislodge ourselves from the world's magnet, but once we start, with God's help, we can slowly move over to His magnet and experience His awesome power. You must also remember, in the end, God's magnet is always the strongest.

THE POWER OF CONTEXT

When I was in college, I spent a few of my

---

[6] Erwin Lutzer, *How to Say No to a Stubborn Habit*, (Colorado Springs, CO: Chariot Victor Publishing, 1994).

Mythinformation - 55

summers working at a small company in Waltham, Massachusetts. Aside from the money, this job provided an unexpected benefit. A large percentage of my co-workers were Spanish-speaking individuals, thus presenting me with a golden opportunity to improve upon the Spanish I had learned in high school.

Though my co-workers were eager to help me out, I often felt a great deal of embarrassment over how poorly I was able to communicate. Certainly, it was much easier for me to understand what others were saying than to try to piece together a sentence myself. Suffice it to say I became a very good listener during those summers.

I quickly learned that the key to understanding what my friends were saying was context. I could piece together long conversations just by understanding a few key words and phrases.

Without a doubt, context reigns supreme in demystification. Understanding the elements that surround a discourse can throw gobs of light on its meaning. Often, context is essential to fully understanding a given form of communication. God's Word is no exception.

A good example of how crucial context can be was once presented to me in a discussion I was having with a friend whom I'll call Lisa. Lisa claimed that the Bible was completely inapplicable to life in the 21st century. I was making some specific references to a particular teaching of the Bible, and she responded, "Yeah, but the Bible also says not to mix certain fabrics! So if we mix polyester and cotton we're sinning! How could that possibly be applicable to life today?" Lisa used this one factoid she had heard as a means for invalidating the

> *"Lisa used this one factoid she had heard as a means for invalidating the entire Bible."*

56 - Permissive Ignorance

entire Bible. Her entire basis was this simple verse.

I looked into Lisa's issue a little more, and found that the verses in the Bible she was referring to were contained in chapter 19 in the book of Leviticus. Specifically, God says, "Do not wear clothing woven of two kinds of material" (Lev. 19:19). Elsewhere in the Bible (context!) it is made clear that the two fabrics that cannot mix are linen and wool. I agree that on its own, this hardly seems a practical piece of wisdom from an all-powerful God.

Let's stop for a second and try to put this in context. The book of Leviticus is the third book of the Bible, and is attributed to Moses. In this book, God is instructing the Israelites on holy living. To begin with, these laws were for the Israelites (that is, the Jewish people). Secondly, as you may know, the Bible is broken up into two major sections: The Old Testament and The New Testament. Here, "testament" means "covenant" or quite simply, an agreement between God and man. Leviticus is a book of the Old Testament, or Old Covenant. So, unless you're Jewish, and presently live sometime before the birth of Christ (that is, before the New Testament), you shouldn't lose sleep over this.

"Understanding the whole Bible, not just one piece, makes a big difference."

Here's where context plays an even bigger role, and understanding the *whole* Bible, not just one piece, makes a big difference. The Jews are God's chosen people; the people through whom He chose to reveal Himself to the world.[7] To this end, God wished the Jews to follow a very specific and rigorous set of laws. To put it in more modern terms, the President of the United States

---

[7] Note that the ultimate revelation of God through the Jewish people was realized in the birth of Jesus Christ.

has numerous aides and assistants to help him with his job. Many of these people are spokespeople and representatives for the President. I'm sure the President demands of these people that they carry themselves in a certain manner: professional, clean, dignified, and with integrity. After all, these people are representing him, and he wants the world to see him as he (hopefully) is.

In essence, this is the same thing God was trying to do through the Jewish people. Naturally, things were on a much larger scale. God wished to show the world his holiness and purity through the Jewish people.

In Mosaic times, linen was a fabric worn by priests, and priestly holiness was thus connected with linen. You can see already that mixing a linen garment with wool symbolically contaminates the clothing. Note also that wool and linen have very different properties. Wool causes people to retain sweat on their bodies, whereas linen does not. The two fabrics are therefore at cross-purposes. Wearing clothing woven from just one fabric, then, comes to symbolize personal purity and a singleness of purpose, i.e., holiness and service to God.

In his book, *The Institutes of Biblical Law*, scholar R.J. Rushdoony states that the issue of wool and linen is for priests in a priestly nation. In Old Testament times, priests were to be from the Jewish tribe of Levi (this is how Leviticus got its name). So this law is for a Jewish Levite. Rushdoony emphasizes as well that the matter was utterly symbolic and ritualistic.[8]

What a difference context makes! Regardless, the Old Covenant has been fulfilled in Jesus; we now live under a New Covenant with God. So wear a wool-linen blend tomorrow, if any exist. There is certainly much more theology to go along with this, but I'll allow you the

---

[8] R. J. Rushdoony, *The Institutes of Biblical Law*, Vol. 1 (Nutley, NJ: Craig Press, 1973), p. 253-62.

opportunity to learn more about the Bible on your own.

The only point I'm trying to make with this example is that context is very important in the Bible, as it is everywhere else in life. I would be gravely mistaken if I were to read one act of *Romeo and Juliet* and assume to know the whole story. The same applies to the Bible. In the book of Psalms, chapter 14, it is written, "there is no God." Does this mean that the Bible teaches the nonexistence of God? Certainly not! Only the whole passage reveals the true meaning, "The fool says in his heart, 'there is no God'" (Ps. 14:1). Context is everything!

Misunderstanding the context of a verse in the Bible has lead to all sorts of pain and suffering in the world. Consider the times you've seen white supremacists on television claiming that their racism is Biblical. How many talk shows have featured married couples wherein husbands treat their wives despicably as slaves because "it's in the Bible?" I agree that many factors contribute to such radical levels of depravity, but much of its root can be traced to a few Bible verses taken out of context.

A NON-RITUALISTIC NON-RELIGION

An important point that I would like to make is that getting caught up in the *religion* of Christianity is a very shaky path to take. Religion is a man made thing, and prone to failure. Christianity is a *relationship* first and a religion second. Christianity is a relationship between you and God through Jesus Christ.

"Christianity is a relationship first and a religion second."

The religion part falls secondary to that. Anybody can be religious, and follow rules, but if you're not rightly related to God, it doesn't matter. I refer to Christianity as a religion in this book only because it is so widely defined as such. A popular Christian quote addresses the matter perfectly: "Religion is man's attempt to reach God; Christianity is God's attempt to reach man."

It is easy to see how many people are let down by Christianity if their only real understanding of it is at a religious level. I remember feeling the same way: do this, don't do that, don't eat this, wear this...who would want to be a part of that? It is unfortunate that so many people focus on all the outward acts of Christianity by being overly legalistic about each detail of their lives. Meanwhile, the more important points are lost.

All the legalism, all the pomp and circumstance, all that seems shallow or flashy is not what Christianity is about at its heart. Don't let that turn you off. Don't let that stop you from researching Christianity. The Christian faith is something far more beautiful, meaningful, and profound than any number of rituals, bylaws, or gold-laced ceremonies man could ever dream up.

"Christianity works from the inside out."

What's more, Christianity works from the inside out. You're rightly related to God through Christ before anything else. The spirit of God dwells within you, *then* you begin to act differently. If I buy my mother flowers, it doesn't mean that I love her. All I did was buy her flowers. It represents my love for her, but it doesn't mean anything. I could begrudgingly hand them to her while thinking to myself, "this will shut her up." My love for her is on the inside first. The outside acts can be done regardless of my inside feelings. When I love her on the inside, my actions will naturally follow, and I'll do things like buy her flowers.

It's the relationship with God that counts, folks.

60 - Permissive Ignorance

Try not to focus on whether or not you can eat an olive on the third Sunday of the fifth month of an odd numbered year when Mars is in retrograde. Nothing is as important to God as your inside feelings towards Him, and your relationship with Him.

I can't write the above paragraph in good conscience without this warning: the fact that your relationship to God is more important than your outward actions does not give the license to sin that some may infer. Many get into trouble this way. I can't consistently lie, steal, miss church, or ignore prayer and Bible study while thinking, "None of that really matters; I love God. It's all outward stuff. God knows that. I have a good heart." Remember, if you confess God is who He claims to be in the Bible, and if you do love Him, you will not do, or even want to do such things. If you love somebody, do you seek to disobey him or her? Are you satisfied with not knowing much about him or her? A resounding "no" should answer on both counts.

Philip Yancey draws an excellent illustration in his book, *What's So Amazing About Grace?* Moments before a young couple is to be married, the husband-to-be says to his future wife, "Darling, I love you, and can't wait to spend the rest of my life with you. Once we're married, though, can I still sleep with other women? How far can I go with another woman before you'll divorce me? Do I have to pay attention to you all the time when you're talking? Remember, I'll always love you on the inside."[9]

It goes without saying that this man deserves a slap in the face. Yancey goes on to say that our relationship with God should be viewed in the same light. True, God's grace is infinite, He loves us no matter what we do, and our relationship with Him is paramount. If

---

[9] Philip Yancey, *What's So Amazing About Grace?* (Grand Rapids, MI: Zondervan, 1997).

we truly love Him, however, we won't try to "get away" with hurting Him or ignoring Him.

Much like a bride and groom, in loving God we seek to please Him, understand Him, listen to Him and be with Him. Like any other relationship, we'll grow to love Him more and more over time. As our love grows, so does our joy in simply knowing Him.

A READING RAINBOW

As a friend and I sat down to dinner one night, we began to speak about Christianity a little bit. I mentioned something about the four Gospels (the books written about the life of Jesus: Matthew, Mark, Luke, and John) and she nearly fell over. "Oh, don't even get me started on the Gospels!" she exclaimed.

"What do you mean?"

"It's just absurd. *Four* Gospels? Why *four*? Why not just one?!?"

It was an interesting way to start a meal. I've heard other people ask this same question. Even more, I know of many who question the validity of the Gospels themselves because they are all unique. I once heard a scholar mention how only three of the four Gospels mention the famous "Last Supper" of Jesus. If the Last Supper was such an important event, why wasn't it mentioned in the fourth Gospel? One Gospel will mention miracles Jesus performs while another Gospel book mentions

"How could these books be accurate if they're so different?"

different ones. This is all a very big mess, isn't it? How could these books be accurate if they're so different? How can they all be accurate if some mention more or less than the others?

In short, the above is a seemingly fantastic way in

which many seek to refute the Christian claim that the Gospels are trustworthy: if the Gospels are not trustworthy, the entire Bible must therefore be held in high suspicion. Let's take a closer look though.

Please consider the notion of a level playing field for a moment. Though I used to be a fantastic advocate against Christianity, one of the things that eventually turned me around was realizing that in my arguments I was demanding more of Christianity than any other doctrine. I wanted more evidence and logic from Christianity than from a non-Christian belief. If the four Gospels aren't exactly the same, does it stand to reason that they must be fraudulent? Or, does this argument demand the unreasonable?

Take four different books about any other famous person and see if they all stress the exact same things, and mention the exact same events in the exact same way. Why hold the Gospel to a different standard? Was only one book written about Einstein? Napoleon? John Lennon? Why is it so unforgivable that four books were written about Jesus?

If you were to grab four biographies written by four different authors about a certain individual, I guarantee that they would be equally different as the Gospels are in telling the story of Jesus' life. Each would stress slightly different aspects of the person's life, perhaps illustrating through different stories. The "big stuff" however would probably be the same, right? In fact, if I read two different books that mentioned with striking similarity all of the same events, I would become highly suspicious that they *were* fraudulent, as the situation

"Take four different books about any other famous person and see if they all stress the exact same things."

certainly suggests that one was copied from the other.

Consider George Washington, our nation's first president. If you find the time, read four books about him, noting the similarities and differences. Do they mention that he was the first president of the United States? Do they agree that he died in 1799? Is Martha Washington his wife in all four books? For sure, the key events, the "big stuff" in George's life are all there.

The four Gospels sure do agree about the "big stuff" concerning Jesus: His death and resurrection are both mentioned. All of them agree Jesus was a righteous man, full of love and compassion, and without sin. Perhaps most importantly, all of them depict Jesus as God incarnate, with Jesus Himself claiming deity. The list could go on and on. There is a beautiful harmony among the four Gospels. It is a wonderful gift from God that we have four Gospels. Four different men, Matthew, Mark, Luke, and John, all wrote about the life and times of Jesus in their unique way, shedding light on the events God wished them to. Putting each unique gospel together helps to create a very full picture of Christ that would be difficult to convey by a single author.

"There is a beautiful harmony among the four Gospels."

Finally, one book mentioning an event that another book doesn't mention is not a contradiction. If Joe writes a book that says Einstein loved apples, and Mary doesn't mention anything about apples at all in her book, does that mean that either Joe or Mary are wrong, or worse yet, liars? Let's take it a step further: Joe says that Einstein loved apples; Mary says that Einstein loved grapes. Is that a contradiction? Could Einstein have loved apples *and* grapes?

Are there questions that the Bible can't directly

64 - Permissive Ignorance

answer? Are there things that are hard to explain? Yes. I'd be lying if I said reading the Bible would neatly wrap up every question and concern you've ever had about life. Find me any other doctrine in the world that has everything explained down to the last question. Unless you're talking about peanut butter and jelly sandwiches, you're not going to find it.

The big stuff, the important stuff, all that a man or woman *needs* to know to live the Christian life is there though, in beautiful harmony. If you flip back to my six-point, working "definition" of Christianity, all of *that* is there, as well as so much more.

There are going to be riddles to which we don't have solutions. There are mysteries God has chosen not to reveal to us yet, and that's where our faith comes into play. We trust that God has things figured out. He has given us all that we *need* to know in the Bible. C.S. Lewis said that the best things are perhaps those that we understand the least. When I try to fathom God's infinite love for us, I have to agree.

Four

❧

Shady Characters

"That there is a Devil is a thing doubted by none but such as are under the influence of the Devil."
-Cotton Mather

Could it be...Satan?!?

This section heading was one of my favorite lines from comedian Dana Carvey when he played the Church Lady (who, by the way, probably fits many of the stereotypes the secular world has about elderly Christian women). Could the fact that you won't accept Jesus Christ be the result of following Satan? The Christian answer is yes. Simply put, if you're not of Christ, you are of Satan. It is black and white.

When we think of serving Satan, we tend to think of the occult: human sacrifice, the black mass, gothic dress, or other unspeakable deeds. Though these certainly fall into the category of serving Satan, few realize that anything other than serving Jesus Christ is in service of the devil.[10]

Let's perform a thought experiment. Pretend that you are Satan, that is, you are completely devoted to working against God (even if you're not a believer of God

---

[10] Please do not infer that because it is not in obvious service to Christ, cooking apple pie is thus serving Satan. The intent here is to be clear that any creed apart from or renounced by Christ, is Satanic.

or Satan yet, just work with me on this). You are utterly evil, and per your villainy, your singular goal is to lead people away from the Truth of God. How would you do it? I assure you that your answers will make up a subset of all the tactics Satan employs to keep people from Christ.

If you wanted to keep people from God, wouldn't you fill the world with a multitude of temptations to which the Godly are forbidden to succumb? Wouldn't you allow hypocrites to give Christianity a bad name? Wouldn't you make the Christian faith unpopular? Wouldn't you exploit every single weakness of the human condition to its fullest? Nothing is too evil or sinister for Satan, so he will use whatever he can to keep you from the truth.

"The best trick Satan ever played was convincing people that he didn't exist."

All of Satan's tactics stem from deceit. That is why Jesus called him "the father of lies." He knows that God is real, and that Jesus is His Son, who rose from the dead for our sins. He knows that the Lord is more powerful than him. He knows that he's already lost the battle against God. Thus, to keep you from God, he lies to you…constantly.

There is an old adage: "The best trick Satan ever played was convincing people that he didn't exist." Most Americans, Christian or otherwise, identify with Satan or the devil as an evil being. Independent of their belief in God or the devil, if you were to tell somebody that they are serving Satan, chances are they wouldn't take it as a compliment. Their response would most likely be one of denial, and an emotional one at that. Some might even laugh, as they conjure up pictures of a goofy looking individual in red tights holding a pitchfork.

Satan knows this, of course. He knows that very

few people want to *consciously* serve him. His solution is to make you think he doesn't exist. He knows that if most nonbelievers were aware of the fact that disbelief in Jesus meant they were servants of the devil, they would change their ways. If you don't believe he exists, though, you can live your life in disbelief of Jesus with a clear conscience.

Better yet, why not make a joke out of it? I can't begin to count all the times I've heard a friend laugh and say, "I'm going straight to Hell." This usually happens after they've done something they know is wrong, or in poor taste. In so many ways Satan and Hell have become big jokes in our society. Hell is even portrayed as just another place where all the fun-loving people will party for eternity. Heaven is for the boring people. There is not even a hint of this notion anywhere in the Bible.

Another tactic employed by Satan is keeping you away from books like the one you're reading now. He doesn't want you to research Christianity, because he doesn't want to lose you. He knows that if you follow my advice, and do the research, you'll be won over to Jesus. His solution? Keep you ignorant.

Hitler was famous for doing the very same thing. He was smart enough to know that knowledge is powerful, and if people were ignorant, or couldn't think for themselves, they would be more apt to follow him. Thus, thousands of books were burned in giant pyres during Nazi rallies. It is a very simple, and remarkably effective tactic. People are easier to control and manipulate when they are ignorant and uneducated.

"Ignorance is the greatest weakness to any person in this society."

Ignorance is the greatest weakness to any person in this society. Your ignorance provides a means for people to take advantage of you. Almost everybody has had an experience when a crooked salesman, mechanic or colleague took advantage of his or her ignorance. If you are ignorant of Christianity, then you open yourself up for the same exploitation, except this time the consequences are much worse than an unreliable car.

Are you allowing yourself "not to think?" Do you shrug off questions about the afterlife, Jesus and God? I believe that the devil spends more time trying to *block* good thoughts from entering our minds, rather than planting bad thoughts. God has given us a conscience. We know what is right and wrong. But, if we can shrug things off, or just not think about them, we're wide open to sin.

I don't think there is a cigarette smoker in the world who believes that smoking is a healthy habit. I will wager that most of them were pulled into their addiction by not thinking about the consequences of their actions. Don't think. Just do it. Worry about it later. It's quite a devious way to lead somebody astray, and the devil excels at it. Don't turn off your brain or ignore your conscience. The consequences can be devastating.

> *"Hitler once said, 'What luck for rulers, that men do not think.'"*

Hitler once said, "What luck for rulers, that men do not think." Hitler, a mere man, was able to coax millions of people from all walks of life to accept his vision of right and wrong. Don't let the same happen to you. Educate yourself and think for yourself. Most of all, *think*. Knowledge is power; knowledge of Christ is even better! Christianity can stand (and has stood) up to the most scrutinizing of investigations. Have at it! Educate yourself; don't allow the devil to keep you ignorant any longer.

ONE PART JESUS, FIVE PARTS WATER

Earlier in this book, I wrote of those who uphold the "happy grandpa" image of God: the God who has the "boys will be boys" attitude about sin, and is quick to sweep our transgressions under the rug. I also mentioned that this picture of God is contrary to His true nature. To elaborate, the "happy grandpa" God is a watered down version of the true God.

The watering down process begins when certain truths about God are considered, for example His boundless love for us, and others are ignored, such as His justice and righteousness. The result is a less than accurate depiction of God that is based upon fancy rather than the Biblical revelation.

The same holds for Jesus Christ. A popular belief held today is that Jesus was a great moral teacher, but only a man. This is a watered down version of Jesus. His great wisdom and teachings are considered, but His claims of deity, His miracles, and His ascension from the grave are not. Even a relaxed reading of the Gospels, however, would clearly indicate that there is no room for this view of Jesus.[11] Moreover, the world has had its share of great moral teachers through the ages, none have come even close to changing our world as Jesus has.

"A popular belief held today is that Jesus was a great moral teacher."

Other diluted forms of Christianity develop when people are selective about what they will believe from the Bible. "I agree with Heaven, but I don't agree with Hell."

---

[11] I intentionally do not authenticate my claims here in keeping with my promise to minimize references to Scripture. However, for readers interested in substantiating this claim along with others found in this section, I would recommend reading the Gospel of John. It's all there.

70 - Permissive Ignorance

"I believe in Jesus, but not as the Son of God." If a selective belief system were employed in other areas of life it would often be found quite impractical. We could not say, "I believe in molecules, but not atoms," because the two are invariably linked to one another. If one is to accept the scientific classification of a molecule, it is crucial to also accept the scientific definition of the atom.

Similarly, I cannot believe the Biblical description of Jesus apart from Him being the Son of God. To believe that Jesus was a great moral teacher, you must believe the Gospel accounts of His life. These same accounts also clearly speak of Him asserting his deity and even predicting His death and Resurrection. They go on to describe literally, and in detail, the very death and Resurrection He predicted. There can be no in-between.

I believe Watered Down Christianity is popular because it affords the believer whatever he or she may wish. I can have the comfort of knowing that there is a God who loves me without the humility of admitting that I am a sinner. I can enjoy the thought of Heaven without taking into account the one way I may get there. To those who water down Christianity I ask, by what authority do you choose to believe in only selected Biblical teachings?

"I cannot believe the Biblical description of Jesus apart from Him being the Son of God."

I cannot mention Watered Down Christianity without also mentioning Contaminated Christianity, because the two are so close in principle. Watered Down Christianity ignores certain Biblical truths. Contaminated Christianity either adds non-Biblical teachings or substitutes Biblical truth with non-Biblical dogma, thus contaminating a purely Biblical view. So-called "Christian cults" fall into this category.

Some common examples of Contaminated Christianity are Mormonism, and Jehovah's Witnesses. Though these groups may claim belief in the Bible, something is different, and that something is an invention of man that leads only to disaster. Contaminated Christians may live righteous lives, and speak volumes of truth, but underneath this veneer are numerous clear contradictions and/or additions to Scripture.

Watered Down and Contaminated Christianity stem from one of two possible sources: ignorance or dissent. I believe that ignorance is the more common of the two. Bible study is essential for understanding Christian beliefs, as it is the basis for the faith. Ignorance of the Bible allows one to fill in the gaps with his or her own notion, just as it allows for misunderstanding. Remember that word context?

Ignorance permeates the Christian world, as well, and can lead to Contaminated Christianity. For instance, though many Christians believe that the Bible says, "God helps those who help themselves," this teaching is not stated in Scripture, nor is it even implied.

Dissent is more obvious than ignorance, because it flatly rejects a teaching of the Bible. "I know the Bible speaks of Jesus' ascension, but I don't believe it." Alternately, dissent may replace a Biblical teaching, "I know the Bible speaks of Jesus' ascension, but I believe He simply lived on in people's minds, not as a physical being." I think that dissent is most prevalent when people confuse what they believe with what they *want* to believe.

> *"'I believe in the Bible' disallows any form of 'except' as an addendum."*

"I believe in the Bible, except..." is immediately a contradictory statement. The clause "I believe in the

Bible" disallows any form of "except" as an addendum. A true understanding of the Bible prohibits the addition, omission or revision of any of its contents. It is all or nothing. What will it be? Are you a Watered Down Christian? Have you manufactured your own version of Christianity? To those who answer in the affirmative, may I encourage you to educate yourself, and study the Bible. The results can be life changing!

A Great Relationship

In the previous chapter, I touched upon some of the stereotypes and prejudices people hold against Christians. One of the points I would like to expound upon now is the people who do fit the stereotypes and prejudices. What of the people who give Christianity a bad name? What of the hypocrites, and self-righteous "prudes?"

When I was in college, I took a class titled "North American Indians." As its name implies, the class focused on the lifestyles and history of native cultures in the North America. Throughout the class, I was deeply disturbed at the terrible persecution these people faced, and continue to face. I assure you, the atrocities you've seen in popular movies such as *Dances with Wolves* barely scratch the surface.

"What of Christianity's shady past?"

Christopher Columbus and his gang were just the beginning. I remember reading one of his journals in which he described what fine slaves the natives would make. He was excited to bring back hundreds of them, in the name of the Holy Trinity, for Spain. I read about slaughter, rape, and torture. In the name of the Holy Trinity? These guys were Christians? Why on earth would I want to be associated with Christianity if it has such a horrendous history?

What of Christianity's shady past? The invasion of North America is just one of many tales wherein men have performed utterly heartless deeds "in the name of Jesus." It's still going on today. There are "Christians" today who harass non-Christians, beat their wives, turn their noses up at the poor, steal, molest, lie, and even murder. What of these self-identified men and women of God who lead utterly sinful lives, but go to church every Sunday and look down their noses at others?

Let me be crystal clear about this issue: I've said before that Christianity is not a religion so much as it is a relationship. Christianity is a relationship between you and the living God through Jesus Christ. Please reread that last sentence. Note the relationship is between *you* and the living God. You. It's between *you* and God. No matter what the condition of the world, *your* attitude towards God and *your* relationship with Him is what is important.

To illustrate, imagine you have a twin brother. Throughout life, you are always respectful of your father, and though you often falter, in your heart, you do your best to obey him. You disagree with him from time to time, but at the end of the day, you trust and love him with all your heart. Your brother, on the other hand, is disrespectful to your father. He puts on an outward appearance of obedience and love, but inside he is deceitful, and does not care about your father at all. When your father's back is turned, he does as he pleases, which hurts your father deeply. He is only out for himself.

> *"The relationship is between you and the living God."*

How does your brother's behavior affect your relationship with your father? Does it mean that it's wrong to love your father? Does it mean that your father does not appreciate your love for him? Does it, in fact, mean anything at all? No! At most, you are angered by your brother's attitudes, and upset that he abuses your father's love. Why then, do so many people think differently when it comes to God?

Truth is truth; facts are facts. Whatever people have done, or continue to do, will never change the truth. I once read a perfect analogy that brings this point home. Suppose, for whatever reason, you don't believe in gravity. You are certain that it is a fictitious force, and the only thing that makes gravity appear to exist is our own imagination. To prove your point, you jump from the top of a tall building. You have no bungee cord or parachute. What do you think will happen to you? Do you think that because you simply don't believe in gravity, it will cease to exist? Of course not! Gravity is a physical law of our universe, and a binding fact of living on this planet. Gravity is truth, no matter what you believe.

"Do you think that disbelief in Jesus Christ makes Him nonexistent?"

Let's take it a step further: suppose I believe in gravity so adamantly that I run around the streets all day tripping people, making them fall on the concrete sidewalks, so they can see the power of gravity. This is cruel for sure, and the laws of gravity certainly in no way mandate that I injure others, but do my actions change the fact that gravity exists in our universe? Do my actions alter the truth of gravity in any way? Again, nothing I can do will change the laws of gravity. The same applies to Christianity.

Do you think that disbelief in Jesus Christ makes Him nonexistent? If you don't believe in God, does that mean when you die something different will happen to you, versus the rest of us? Your choice to believe in Jesus has no bearing on whether or not He is real.

If I do wretched things in the name of Christianity, does that change or affect it? If I'm a hateful "Christian", committing any number of black deeds, does that make Jesus Christ different? No and no. It seems to me that many people turn away from Christ because of a bad experience, or series of experiences with a believer: an abusive or domineering nun, a harsh Bible study teacher, a sinful pastor, a hypocritical neighbor. Don't turn from God to spite them. You will only be hurting yourself.

Again, I urge you: please don't let the deeds of others keep you from Jesus. Believing in Him does not mean you must put all other Christians on a pedestal, or condone their behavior. Believing in Jesus means that *you* are saved. Allow God to deal with the deeds of others.

TOLERANCE ≠ INDIFFERENCE

In recent months the word "tolerance" has been a regular on my list of words that I find particularly vexing. This isn't because I dislike tolerance itself, but rather because I feel that it is often a misunderstood concept. It is one I find myself struggling to get my arms around more than I care to admit. Worst of all for tolerance, however, is that it spends so much time being compared to its evil twin brother, "intolerance."

> *"One cannot be tolerant of something without first objecting to it."*

Of paramount importance to understanding tolerance is that one cannot be tolerant of something without first objecting to it. For instance, I am not tolerant of people with blue eyes. Quite contrary, I am quite accepting of people with blue eyes. I could even take it a step further and say that I'm pretty well indifferent to another person's eye color. Either way, I am not tolerant, since I have no objection to people with blue eyes.

If you'll allow me to up the ante a bit, the same can be said of more "hot button" issues in society today. If a man or woman has no objection to abortion (i.e., "it's not my business"), they cannot rightfully be said to be tolerant of abortion. They are indifferent, not tolerant. I feel that this is an important distinction.

The distinction between tolerance and indifference is important because today, the word "intolerance" seems too often used to describe Christians and their behavior. Holding fast to a belief or principle is not intolerance. For instance, I believe with all my heart that Jesus Christ is the Son of God and the singular way to salvation. Some might say that I am therefore intolerant of other religions and world views. This is a harsh, baseless accusation, and a great conversation killer.

"The distinction between tolerance and indifference is important."

It seems to me that those who accuse others of intolerance are really just angry that the accused embrace a different view. The same people will go on to claim I am forcing my values on them, when in fact they are more than willing to do the same on some other issue.

Here comes the rub: true tolerance mandates that I choose to withhold any means I might have to force my way on someone else's behavior. I officially step over the line and become intolerant when I begin to coerce others, rather than persuade them. Closely associated with intolerance is anger. In fact, my dictionary uses the word anger in its definition of intolerant.

A few years ago, I participated in an AIDS walk in

Boston. This charity event raised monies for people living with AIDS. Funds were used to offset the cost of medication, and help researchers find a cure. A few miles into the walk, I passed by three men holding up signs for passersby. I do not wish to recount the words on these signs, but all of them said essentially the same thing: God hates homosexuals, and all homosexuals are going to Hell.

Quite candidly, these men embarrassed me. Their actions make me both angry and sad. I am in no position to judge them, for sure, but I adamantly disagree with their demonstration. Two things tip me off about this demonstration: hate and judgment.

In the Bible, Jesus is crystal clear when it comes to judging others: don't. Equally clear is His message about how we are to relate to others: with love. Christians are not called by God to be tolerant of others, but rather, to love others. I thus file away any actions of hate, resentment, exclusion, or judgment as positively contrary to God's intentions for our lives.

It is not wrong that these men believe homosexual activity is a sin. Even more, the men displayed tolerance. In my opinion their demonstration was quite distasteful, and very inappropriate. It really makes me cringe. However, they were not forcing their way upon others, but rather trying to persuade them. (I don't doubt, however, that their efforts were a complete failure.) Regardless, theirs was a tolerant demonstration.

> *"Jesus is crystal clear when it comes to judging others: don't."*

I'm sad to say that Christianity is littered with such people who have the crazy notion that judging people and telling them that God hates them will bring them into the Christian fold. Folks, this is everywhere. Hypocrisy, hatred, judgment, double standards, and intolerance are everywhere. They are found in the far left, the far right, and everywhere in between. No group is devoid of shady characters. Every religion, every political party, every conglomerate, and every social movement has them.

I fear that the discussions on the rights or wrongs of protesting or voicing opinions will never end. On one hand, Christians are called to preach the Gospel, and many feel called to alert others who may be practicing certain sins to the error in their ways. There is nothing wrong with calling others to repentance. On the other hand, the world seems far too short on grace, compassion and respect. I believe the bridge between these poles is love. There is a world of difference between patiently, lovingly, and humbly rebuking an individual and yelling out "sinner!" Christians would be wise to adopt the former as their method of choice.

To me, this is all peripheral activity to what should be our principal pursuit: Jesus Christ. Jesus said "follow me," and that's what I'm going to try to focus on. We will never be wanting for other important issues upon which to direct our energies. Our job is to decide what's most important. I believe that a humble, sincere and fervent pursuit of Christ is paramount, and will disappoint no one. There are many other important issues out there, but they can come after Christ.

Tolerance will remain one of my least favorite words, I am afraid. But again, we are brought to the same point: what about Jesus? What about the Bible? The deeds of others or the issues that surround Christianity have no affect on who Jesus Christ is, or what the Bible says. God is far above all these things, and it is upon Him that we should fix our gaze in the pursuit of Truth.

Five

ଓ

Your Little Secrets

"We should not be ashamed to name what God has not been ashamed to create."
-Clement of Alexandria

United We Stand

At the beginning of this book, you read that my break from Christianity began as I started to get older and take on more responsibilities. For me, this time was high school. I became too focused on "living my life" to worry about religion. Even further from my mind was death! Slowly but surely, the world pulled me in deeper and deeper: girls to think about, tests to study for, money to earn, colleges to apply to, girls to think about...

Religion became a novelty that made for an interesting discussion over a drink with friends. My religion had become whatever was convenient for me. I wouldn't allow it to get in the way of my desires in "the real world." A doctrine such as "don't kill anybody," for instance, was easily incorporated into my religion. "Don't have sex until you are married," however, got in the way of what I wanted, thus I found some means of disqualifying it.

I was deceiving myself. I was keeping myself dumb and happy through some shallow, uninformed generalizations, which allowed me to live my life as I saw fit. As I made these choices, relics of my Christian

80 - Permissive Ignorance

upbringing would cry out in protest. The arguments went something like this:

> *Non-Christian Brian:* I want to do "X."
> *Christian Brian:* You really shouldn't. God forbids "X."
> *Non-Christian Brian:* Does He really, though? How do you know?
> *Christian Brian:* The Bible says so.
> *Non-Christian Brian:* Yeah, but the Bible was written thousands of years ago. It's not applicable today. Plus, man has probably manipulated it over the years anyway. At a minimum, it's misinterpreted.
> *Christian Brian:* What about the commandment to honor your mother and father? I know you believe in that. They certainly wouldn't approve of this...
> *Non-Christian Brian:* Perhaps, but I am an adult now, and no longer in their care. I can make my own decisions. They were brought up in a different age, with different morals.
> *Christian Brian:* But doesn't it make sense that God wouldn't allow "X?" It could be dangerous, after all.
> *Non-Christian Brian:* No way. Why would God make "X" so much fun? Why deny myself the pleasure? Why would God make us like this? Either God doesn't exist, and didn't make us in the first place, or God has no issue with "X." No other option makes sense. How could I be doing something wrong? Who's getting hurt? It's not like I'm killing somebody...

And that was that. "Christian Brian" lost the arguments again and again. The fact that I needed to rationalize my choices to myself meant I was dealing with an inner conflict. Somewhere, there was a warning bell ringing in my head. Making a decision from inner conflict meant that I had to sacrifice peace of mind. I would second guess myself after a questionable act, and wonder if I did the right thing. My solution to this problem was just to stop thinking about it. Slowly, the conflicts would go away, until the voice of "Christian Brian" was barely audible. The more and more I let "Non-Christian Brian" win, the stronger he became.

"Making a decision from inner conflict meant that I had to sacrifice peace of mind."

(Remember the magnet example?) In a short time, I wouldn't even question "X."

Have you ever felt conflict about some of the choices you've made? Have you ever listened to your inner voices quibble? Usually, one of them wants to do what is easier, quicker, or more pleasurable, while the other takes the moral stand; the option that doesn't provide instant gratification or pleasure. What do you think is generating that conflict? Don't you feel as if you should resolve it first? Wouldn't it be nice to have peace of mind in the decisions you make?

Believe it or not, one of the voices in your head is your conscience. It is the conscience that God gave you. It is His voice, quietly urging you to do the right thing. This is possibly the same voice that convinced you to read this book, even though another part of you didn't want to. This is the same voice that makes you feel badly when you do something wrong. Do you think it's coincidental that most people would agree that murder, theft, and lying are wrong? Regardless of whether or not they succumb to these crimes, most feel guilt for their wrongs. Those without remorse have just learned to deny their conscience. In the same way that I was able to quiet the voice of "Christian Brian," so can anybody silence his or her conscience.

How many times in your life have you been reminded of the fact that doing the right thing always works out for the best? How many times has the quicker, easier path been more rewarding in the long haul? How many people do you know who have regrets about doing the right thing? Years later, does anybody regret being honest, or doing what is honorable and good? What do you usually hear when people have regrets? "I wish I didn't lose my temper." "I wish I had been more patient." "I shouldn't have lied." "I should have stayed faithful." "Getting into drugs was the biggest mistake of my life." We don't regret doing right, folks. Maybe we regret the short-term consequences, but down the road, it always feels better. Lou Holtz, perhaps one of the most renowned collegiate football coaches and motivators, always urges his audience, "do right!"

"How many people do you know who have regrets about doing the right thing?"

Most of the time, we know what is right and wrong, because our conscience tells us so. We don't have to justify our actions to ourselves or anybody else when we do what's right. I'm sure there have been times in your life when you have done something that may not have been pleasant at first. It always works out for the best, though. God's plan for us is the same.

Some of the people I've spoken to about God hesitate before they will deny Him out loud. They'll claim disbelief in Jesus, but feel some discomfort actually saying it. Again, something is crying out to them. Something inside them is saying, "Be careful! Watch what you say! Are you sure? What if you're wrong?"

Have you ever heard that voice? Do you feel comfortable proclaiming, in an audible voice, that you reject the teachings of Jesus? That you deny the existence of God? Before you say it in spite of me, let me warn you: this is no joke.

Billy Graham, one of the world's most renowned evangelists, has literally touched millions of lives for Christ. Of the thousands he's met and spoken to, Mr. Graham says "I have never met a person who came to Christ late in life who didn't wish they had come much, much sooner."[12] Come to Christ, and set your mind at ease.

"This is no joke."

ARE YOU A CLOSET CHRISTIAN?

In 1980, at the tender age of six, I had open-heart surgery due to a genetic defect with one of the valves in my heart. At the time, this was a very serious operation with potential consequences ranging from brain damage to death if not successful.

One of the more vivid memories I have of that time took place during the morning of my operation. The nurses came to prep me in my hospital room, while my parents stood close by. I was strapped down on a gurney, and pushed to an elevator that would carry me down to the operating room. I remember looking up at my parents in the elevator, and knowing that something was wrong. They weren't the happy parents I was used to seeing. I could tell they were struggling with pain on some level.

Due to my age, I couldn't comprehend what my parents were suffering, nor could I understand the effect the next few hours would have on my life. All I knew was

---

[12] Billy Graham, *My Answer*, http://www.billygraham.org, June 7, 2001.

that something was terribly wrong, because my parents, my infallible heroes, were upset. Soon the elevator stopped, and the nurse started to push me away. Now something was definitely wrong. I began to cry. I thought I was being taken away from my parents forever. I had no idea what was going on.

Even today, I feel a lump form in my throat as my parents describe to me what it was like to see their youngest child being pushed away from them towards the operating room that day. I was waving good-bye to them with one hand and clutching my favorite teddy bear with the other. It very well could have been the last time they saw me alive.

> *"Saying a prayer on the best day of our lives seems ludicrous."*

In the hours that followed, my mother and father walked to a local church, where they prayed until the operation was finished. As they put it, "We prayed to God with all our heart and soul." To their relief, the operation was a success, their prayers were answered, and my heart has been healthy ever since. The issue of brain damage, however, is still hotly contested within the Marchionni household.

When times are good, and we have little to worry about, it is easy to forget that we need God in our lives. Furthermore, it is easier to deny that He even exists. Saying a prayer on the best day of our lives seems ludicrous. We're in control! We've got life all figured out! We're powerful and on top of the world! We're a success!

When faced with great adversity, or something we don't think we can handle, however, saying a prayer suddenly isn't as ridiculous as it once seemed. When something very important to us seems completely out of our control, God is quickly brought back into our lives, just in case. Perish the thought, but if you were placed in a situation similar to what my parents experienced, what would you do? Would you pray to God?

I like to call this duplicity the "foul-weather-friend" complex. Simply put, when times are tough, God is our best buddy. If things are going well, who needs Him? Earlier in this book, I talked about the inner division some of us face when making decisions; how we sometimes have arguments with ourselves over a certain issue. The foul-weather-friend complex is just another form of this division. A warning bell is going off in your head again, except this time you're listening to it, because you're not feeling so good anymore.

"When times are tough, God is our best buddy."

No experience in my life has cemented this concept in my mind more than the events of September 11, 2001. The tragedy of that day remains beyond my capacity to grasp, or even put into words. Truly that day has unalterably changed the lives of millions, and will continue to affect men, women and children well beyond the newspaper headlines, celebrity fund-raisers, and memorial dedications.

America, as well as many other parts of the world, is clearly changed because of this day. One notable change was how common the words "God" and "prayer" became in everyday vernacular. In minutes, offering to pray for somebody, or mentioning God was no longer a ridiculous or embarrassing concept, rather, it was prevalent, and even encouraged.

The fact that so many are able to cast doubt aside for a few moments and pray to God suggests that their disbelief in Him may not be as strong as they might purport. It is amazing how adversity will soften our stubbornness to believe. Sometimes, I believe that God allows adversity in our lives simply so we will come to realize our need for Him.

If you find yourself living this double standard, don't you think it might be worth exploring? Where did people turn after September 11? Did Americans seek out the atheists, skeptics, and champions of the secular world? Or, did they look to the priests, pastors, or other Godly men and women?

When I've heard people relate a crisis or emergency story to me, often they will mention how they found themselves praying when they were at their lowest, or most desperate: "God, I don't know if you're real, but if you are, please help me through this." These people are actually expressing an inkling of faith in God. There is just a tiny fragment of faith there, that God is actually hearing their prayer, and that He will have mercy on them. Coincidentally, a tiny fragment of faith is all you need to begin your Christian walk.

"A tiny fragment of faith is all you need to begin your Christian walk."

Many will even try to bargain with God: "If you help me now, I promise that I'll go to church, be a better person, or do whatever you want!" This is a scary place to be, for sure. I would suggest to any who have been there to closely examine their attitude towards God. Perhaps you believe in Him, or even *want* to believe in Him more than you think.

Have you ever prayed "just in case?" If you have ever been so compelled to pray "just in case" God is real, or "just in case" the Bible is true, why aren't you looking into Christianity "just in case" your eternal destiny is in God's hands? If a crisis situation can frighten you enough to pray to the Lord "just in case," why aren't you a full time believer? Why not research that a little bit "just in case" your life after death is headed in the wrong direction? I assure you, your worst travesty here on earth would pale in comparison to eternal damnation, just as your greatest earthly joy won't be able to hold a candle to a moment in Heaven.

"WHY GOD?"

When hardship comes our way, or when we see the suffering of others, we cannot help but ask, "Why God? Why have you allowed this to happen?" I doubt there is a person alive today that hasn't asked this question in some form. It is part of the human condition to wonder why things are as they are. Our need for explanation seems to grow especially strong when we are beset by tragedy or hardship.

Though I think it natural to question why certain things happen, I often wonder why this seems most prevalent during hardship. Why does not the human race cry "why God?" in the midst of happiness, or during prosperity? When was the last time you heard, "Why God? Why have You allowed me to be so prosperous? Why am I so healthy right now? Why have You provided food for me?"

It seems to me that God is questioned through difficult times and discounted during prosperous times. When we are in trouble, scrutinizing God, His motives, or even His existence comes quite naturally. On the contrary, when we are doing well, and feel happiness, or experience any good fortune, there is no God.

"God is questioned through difficult times and discounted during prosperous times."

He isn't even taken into account. "Why God?" becomes "What God?" "I earned this. I deserve this. What God? There is no God. This is just good luck; the reward due to me for my hard work."

Verily, in many ways God seems to get the worst of both worlds: blame or questioning during the bad, and neglect during the good. I doubt humankind will ever be able to stop wondering "why God?" during times of tragedy. It is too ingrained in our nature. However, through His work in our lives, we can begin trust Him, even though we may not understand. Even more, perhaps we could spare a moment to say "Thank you God" when we have been blessed.

ARE YOU USING ATHEISM AS A CRUTCH?

Those with the "foul-weather friend" syndrome tend to turn to God only in times of need. Since they believe in Him at their weakest, and most helpless, it is easy to see how many believe that people who are always turned to God must always be needy, or weak. Hence the popular theory that Christianity, or religion in general, is just a crutch for those unable to handle the world on their own. In actuality, I think the crutch works the other way.

Simply put, atheism is a crutch, too. Non-belief provides a justification for living your life exactly how you want to, answering to nothing and no one. You need not bend a knee to anybody if you don't want to. You need this "crutch" of disbelief otherwise you would have to change your life style, as you would no longer be able to validate or rationalize the way you are living.

"Atheism is a crutch, too."

"But what if I'm already leading a good life?" is a response I hear frequently "I don't need a crutch to justify how I'm living, because I'm a good person. I already have good morals, why do I need to believe in God?" Though an interesting point, there is a key difference: you are the one making the rules. Whether the rules are good or bad is inconsequential. You are putting yourself at the helm either way; you make your own rules, instead of submitting to God's. So the "crutch" remains, though hidden by this rationalization.

Also worth mentioning is the simple fact that we need a crutch. This is much harder to remember when times are good, and we're not faced with any great difficulties or tragedies. It is a hard world, and we need crutches. One of the most important needs any human being has is the need to feel loved. All our lives we seek acceptance and love from others. Isn't this a crutch? Haven't you ever wanted a shoulder to cry on? Have you ever sought advice? Do you think you could have made it to where you are now without the help of all the crutches you have in your life? Think of all the troubles you have overcome. I'll bet you had your share of crutches to help you through: family, friends, your spouse, perhaps even a pet that was a special comfort to you.

"Jesus is more than a crutch for us."

Finally, calling the belief in Christ an emotional crutch doesn't do it justice. Jesus is more than a crutch for us. In his excellent book *A Ready Defense*, Josh McDowell says that calling Christianity a crutch is like a light bulb saying to its socket, "You are my crutch."[13] We need Jesus to live within us to be truly alive, hence the Biblical expression, "to live in Christ." He is more than our crutch; He is the center of our lives, and truly lights us up. Just as a light bulb was made to function properly in its socket, so were we made to function properly in a relationship with God through Jesus Christ.

---

[13] Josh McDowell, *A Ready Defense*, (Nashville, TN: Thomas Nelson Publishers, 1993).

HONESTY SHOULDN'T BE SO LONELY

Have you ever noticed that when you are looking for a certain answer to a question, you are often able to find it? This usually happens when you ignore, consciously or unconsciously, certain details about the question or situation. When it comes to matters of self, you must be deceitful in order to do this. The person you are deceiving is yourself. It is difficult to recognize as deception because it seems so innocent. Your mind wants to ignore a certain truth, so as a protection mechanism, it finds a way to invalidate that truth, and generate an answer that is more palatable. It is perhaps easier to deceive ourselves than anybody else.

"The person you are deceiving is yourself."

Humans seem most prone to this sort of behavior when a certain conclusion demands admission of a personal fault, or a change in lifestyle. Though it may temporarily protect your ego, self-deceit is probably the greatest disservice you could ever do to yourself. Think of how important honesty is in a relationship with friends and loved ones. Don't you owe yourself the very same?

If I have the luxury of time, one of the most effective ways I know of to stay true to myself is to make a slow decision. Should you find yourself considering Christianity, be sure to give yourself ample time to think everything through. Though it is still possible to deceive yourself, and find the answer you want, it's much harder if you stew on it for a while. It's almost impossible to outsmart yourself if you give all the checks and balances in your brain time to have their say. As you'll see in the next section, a little extra "stew time" is often sorely needed.

POPPIN' FRESH FIRE

One of my favorite snacks is popcorn. When I make popcorn, I prefer to do it the old-fashioned way: I put some oil in a pot, heat it up, and then put the corn in. I sprinkle a little salt on top and then I'm ready for a good movie. It's a relatively healthful snack, and easy to make. Thus ends my unsolicited commercial for popcorn.

My first experience with making popcorn, however, was less than successful. Allow me to relate to you the first in a series of stories I'll use to fill my next book, *Memoirs of a Dumb Bachelor*.

When I was twenty-four, I was out food shopping and saw some fancy, organic, "super-hybrid popping corn" in the supermarket. Sold! I rented a good movie, and couldn't wait to prepare my new, scientifically advanced snack. The instructions on the package said to place one kernel of corn in a few tablespoons of oil, listen for a pop, and then add the rest. I poured some olive oil into a pot and dropped in the kernel. With all of my culinary savvy, I decided to turn the heat onto the highest setting. The oil has to be very hot to make popcorn, right? Of course. So I turned the burner to the highest setting, and waited to hear that first pop.

"I nearly lost my eyebrows as three-foot high flames leapt out of the pan."

I was watching some TV in the other room for a few minutes, and still hadn't heard a pop. I got up and went to the kitchen to check on my forthcoming snack. I took the lid off the pot and nearly lost my eyebrows as three-foot high flames leapt out of the pan. Wups. Now, my inept mind had to devise a solution to the problem at hand: what exactly does one do with a flaming pot in a two-bedroom, third floor apartment with no fire extinguisher?

Nearly everybody to whom I told this story said I should have just put the lid of the pot back on, suffocating the flames. Brilliant. In spite of years of schooling in the sciences, this slick solution escaped me. It's funny how a raging fire on your stove can quickly shut off the more intelligent parts of your brain and throw your survival gear into overdrive.

What did I do? Since my apartment was rapidly filling with smoke, I ran to pull the screeching smoke alarm out of the socket. First things first, right? Next, my agile mind decided the only viable solution was to pick up the flaming pot, and carry it outside onto my balcony.

I grabbed the uncomfortably warm handle, and holding it in front of me, began to walk out to my balcony. Apparently it wasn't enough for me to be an arm's length from a raging fire. I wanted the flames to blow towards me as well. Realizing this after about two steps, I turned around, and walked *backwards* through my apartment, out of my kitchen, through my living room, to my sliding doors—complete with curtains—and out to the balcony. This is the same balcony that is covered entirely in outdoor carpeting.

> *"An elegantly simple solution may exist to a problem."*

Enter stupid decision number four, in case you were counting. I put the flaming pot down on the carpet. At the time I must have subconsciously wanted to create a black circle of incinerated carpeting to add some flare to my balcony's decor. As an added bonus, I could release the carcinogenic fumes of melted plastic. What a perfect ending to a perfect batch of popcorn.

Now, what happened here? Please hold any responses containing the word "idiocy." I bare my soul, and share this story with you to drive home a simple point: sometimes an elegantly simple solution may exist to a problem, but we are too panicked or ignorant to think of it. I could have ended the whole episode by simply covering the pot, and turning off the heat. Given more time, I might have been able to either think of the solution myself, or at a minimum, call up a qualified friend and ask their opinion.

The moral here is not to panic at the first sight of difficulty in your search to discover the truth about Christianity. In my situation with the popcorn, I didn't have any time to think. You do. You can afford to look into things more deeply. You can talk to other Christians. This doesn't mean that you should take a relaxed attitude towards getting your questions answered. What it

"Be careful not to panic and give up when you can't find an answer right away."

does mean is that you have to be careful not to panic and give up when you can't find answers right away.

Christianity has been around for a very long time. It has touched people from every walk of life. The odds that you have found the question or questions that completely rip it apart are about as close to nil as you can get. The answers are out there, and there are many ways to get them. It will not happen overnight, though. It took my friend Randy over a year, and he continues to grow each day. I maintain that it took me ten years, and I'm still growing in faith, too. For others, it only takes a few weeks. Persistence and patience are important qualities in this realm. Remember, there is no more important endeavor. So much is at stake.

Take solace in the fact that God (believe in Him or not), will be helping you. He wants you to find the Truth. He wants you to know Him. If you do believe in God, ask Him for help. Though nobody can claim to know the

94 - Permissive Ignorance

mind of God, I believe that this is an endeavor He will certainly help you complete to satisfaction. Also, remember there are millions of Christians, myself included, who pray for you every night and day.

Six
ಬ
All About Answers

"Nothing in the world is more dangerous than a sincere ignorance and conscientious stupidity."
-Martin Luther King, Jr.

The Answer

There are a series of science fiction books written by Douglas Adams. The first of these is titled *The Hitchhiker's Guide to the Galaxy*. In this book, a group of people build a massive super-computer to help them answer *the* question: the question of "life, the universe, and everything." The computer thinks the question through for many years and finally comes back with the answer, "forty-two." Needless to say, everybody was very disappointed! As the book continues, the people express their displeasure with the computer's answer. He replies that the answer is indeed correct. The problem is that nobody truly understands the *question*. Though intended to be comical, the book touches upon one of the most fundamental characteristics of the human condition: we want answers! Sometimes, however, we aren't even sure which questions we want answers to.

I ended the first chapter of this book with a series of questions. One of the questions I asked was "what do you think you are searching for?" I told you to think about it for a while. Did you come up with an answer?

96 - Permissive Ignorance

I'll bet that many of you can't truly put your finger on what you're searching for in life, or what specific questions you want answered. Perhaps you describe what you want with nonspecific and vague terms like "happiness" or "fulfillment." Some of you may point to numerous worldly concepts: "a meaningful relationship," "a rewarding career," etc. You're probably also searching for the answers to the big questions of "life, the universe and everything."

I know you've heard this before, but in my opinion, you can't hear it enough: Christianity has the answers for you. Not only does it have answers, but they are the only correct answers to some of the toughest questions you have. If you really want to know the best way to live your life, you needn't look further than the Bible.

Here is a research project you might enjoy: interview some of your older friends and relatives, the older the better. Ask them how they feel about their lives. What are they proud of? What do they regret, if anything? How would they feel if their life were demanded of them tomorrow? Expectant? Fulfilled? Scared? Make note of which people look back on their life with peace and fulfillment, and which people look back with regrets and disorder.

"You needn't look further than the Bible."

Though I don't know your circle of friends, relatives or acquaintances, I can almost guarantee that those who believe in Christ, and have sought Him out, even recently, will be the ones who feel most at peace with their life and death. They are the ones who found what they were searching for. Those who are bitter, afraid, or even offended at speaking of death, are most likely not in a relationship with Jesus.

In fact, bitterness is the perhaps the most common

sentiment I sense when I read anti-Christian literature. The tone is sardonic, contemptuous, spiteful, and angry. Is this attitude the hallmark of the nonbeliever? Read a few anti-Christian web sites and decide for yourself. Is theirs the mind-set you wish to acquire?

What are you searching for? The Christian answer is God. You've been searching for God in your life since you were able to think. In your search, you may have even created many gods to take His place: money, sex, drugs, power, the arts, sports, your career, even yourself. Which of these do you believe to be the ultimate answer for you? Do you truly believe that your inner peace and fulfillment will come from anything of this world?

Think of all the stories you've heard of people who have seemed to "have it all" in our world. Have you ever heard anybody with great wealth say that money has kept them happy and fulfilled? Take, for example, many of the celebrities in Hollywood. If you take a hard look at American culture, it is amazing how much influence these people have on our society. They are often looked upon as gods; people who have it all. Americans become obsessed with them; entire magazines and television shows are devoted to poring over the minutiae of their lives. We let them play by an entirely different set of rules.

"What are you searching for? The Christian answer is God."

I certainly looked upon many of them in this way. They had everything I had ever hoped for: a fantastic job, tremendous wealth, power, looks, influence, and so on. Would you say that any of these people are free of problems? Do you believe that they have inner peace? Perhaps some do, but think of the countless stories we hear to the contrary. How many struggle with addictions? How many celebrities have died of a drug overdose, or been slaves to alcoholism? How many stories have you seen on VH-1 or E! that document the tragic life and death of somebody who appeared to have it all? How many have committed suicide, or died alone in misery and seclusion? How many successful marriages are there between celebrities? How many successful families? Do you really believe that these people have it all? Study the lives of Karen Carpenter, Elvis Presley, John Bonham, Marilyn Monroe, Billie Holliday, Andy Gibb, Keith Moon, Kurt Cobain, Donald Simpson, and Jimi Hendrix. Think of the laundry list of celebrities with the most distressing of destructive habits and attitudes.

At best, I would say that the percentage of celebrities or "have it all's" who are truly happy, content, and at peace with life and death in America is equal to the percentage of the rest of us who are. There is no difference. These people are just as happy, or miserable, as the rest of us. They all have problems, doubts, and fears quite similar to our own. The evidence is overwhelming. The evidence would even suggest that the less we have, the less focused we are on worldly matters, the happier we are!

Somehow we remain deceived. We still search for answers everywhere other than where we should be looking. Why? The answer is simple: it's easy. It's easy to live as the world does, and focus on things like money, power, or fame. It's easy to succumb to peer pressure. It's easy to sin. We are easily ensnared by all of its false promises. We like quick answers, and instant gratification. Most of all, it's easy to come up with excuses to reject Christianity. Taking the easy way through life reminds me of a quote from an

"There are two paths to take: One is easy, and this is its only reward."

unknown author: "There are always two paths to take: One is easy, and this is its only reward."

People have been coming up with reasons to reject Christianity for over 2,000 years; you would not be the first. Some of those people, however, have turned around, and seen the Truth. Some of them have even written books about it.

Twelve-step recovery programs, such as Alcoholics Anonymous, stress the importance of belief and dependence on God.[14] In fact, six of the twelve steps to recovery deal directly with God and the addict's relationship to Him. The Alcoholics Anonymous "Big Book" has this to say to the atheist and agnostic:

Everybody nowadays, believes in scores of assumptions for which there is good evidence, but no perfect visual proof. And does not science demonstrate that visual proof is the weakest proof? It is being constantly revealed, as mankind studies the material world, that outward appearances are not inward reality at all. To illustrate:

The prosaic steel girder is a mass of electrons whirling around each other at incredible speed. These tiny bodies are governed by precise laws, and these laws hold true throughout the material world. Science tells us so. We have no reason to doubt it. When, however, the perfectly logical assumption is suggested that underneath the material world and life as we see it, there is an All Powerful, Guiding, Creative Intelligence, right there our perverse streak comes to the surface and we laboriously set out to convince ourselves it isn't so. We read wordy books and indulge in windy arguments, thinking we believe this universe needs no God to explain it. Were our contentions true, it would follow that life originated out of nothing,

---

[14] Note that most of these programs are spiritual in nature, not religious, and thus use "God" to mean "God as you [the program member] understand Him."

means nothing, and proceeds nowhere.[15]

THE DEPARTMENT OF REDUNDANCY DEPARTMENT

I would like to conclude this section by repeating myself. What are you searching for? Are you making an educated decision about the Christian faith? Have you done the research? Or, are you afraid of doing the research? Deep down, I think most people are afraid. As I stated early on in this book, most people don't *want* to believe.

"Do not let society make this decision for you."

Somewhere inside, you know that if you do the research, you may see the Truth, and you might have to change your life. Furthermore, you see the change you will have to make as one for the worse.

I have done my best to break down many of these fears and misconceptions, but ultimately, when you put this book down, the decision is yours. Think about what you're searching for. Are you looking for a belief system that will fit nicely into your present lifestyle, or are you searching for Truth?

Please, reader, please do not let society make this decision for you. Don't let somebody else tell you to refuse Jesus Christ. Don't make this choice in ignorance. Make an educated decision based on evidence, testimony, and fact. Get out there and find out about the Christian faith. Talk to Christians, read the books, read the testimonies, dispel the myths, and get your questions answered and your issues addressed.

Are you going to deny Christ because you saw a two-hour special by some media giant who suggested He wasn't the Son of God? Is that what you're going to hang

---

[15] Alcoholics Anonymous World Services, Inc., *Alcoholics Anonymous* (New York, NY, 1976), 3rd ed., p. 48-49.

your hat on? A few professors who think Christianity is garbage? Some conversations you've had which seem to make sense? Maybe you've read a book or two. Is that it? Is that all you're going to hang your eternity on?

Many of you may turn the question around, "Well Marchionni, am I supposed to just believe you, and hang my hat on that? Am I supposed to just listen to a few Christians and be sold?" A thousand times over I scream, "No!" I'd certainly like it if you believed me right out of the gate, but, to be fair, you shouldn't. I'm saying you should do the research. This is important stuff. Explore it for yourself! Dig in! Read the books for and against Christianity. Most importantly, read lots of them. Then make your decision.

"Are you looking for a belief system that will fit nicely into your present lifestyle, or are you searching for the Truth?"

I assure you, all the evidence you would ever need and more is there. The Christian faith is rational, and watertight. It is the Truth, and it makes sense. If you don't believe me, I encourage you with all of my might to try to prove me wrong.

Put Christianity on trial. I challenge you to disprove the testimony of millions who have been completely changed by Jesus Christ. I challenge you to prove the Bible is full of lies. Bring me all the people you know whose lives changed for the better once they rejected Christianity. You may not find many.

Do you know how many books have begun intending to disprove Christianity and wound up being pro-Christianity? Why do you think that is? Because anything else doesn't hold water. You don't need to trust me, the billions who believe, or the billions who have believed. All you need to do is investigate. Put forth some effort; I'm sure you'll be happy with the results.

Ultimately, matters of spirituality and belief come down to personal choices. We choose to explore Christianity, we choose to follow Christ, we choose to believe in Him. Belief in Jesus isn't something that happens independent of our own will, it is a choice we make.

Reflect on your beliefs. They are all choices. Let's look again at the sub-atomic world. I believe in the scientific notion that all matter is composed of atoms, and that each of these consists of sub-atomic particles: protons, neutrons, and electrons. I choose to believe that these exist. I have never seen them with my own eyes, nor can they be seen. My understanding of their existence and behavior is based almost entirely on the opinions, research, and theories of other men and women. I have seen their behavior on a large scale, but I do not claim to fully understand them. For those readers who are familiar with quantum theory, you'll recall how counter-intuitive and difficult sub-atomic behavior is. Simply put, I must take their existence on some faith. My faith is put in the hands of physicists, mathematicians, chemists, and other scientists who devote their lives to atomic study.

"Ultimately, matters of spirituality and belief come down to personal choices."

The point of this is that I choose to believe. Similarly, my faith in Jesus as the Son of God who died for my sins is a choice. I do not understand all of it, and I never will. I cannot know the mind of God by definition: a finite being cannot grasp the infinite. Still, I have chosen to believe in God, though I haven't seen Him with my eyes.

Some of my faith is based upon the work of others,

but even more is based upon my personal experience. Here, my faith in atoms and my faith in God depart. The better half of my faith in atoms is based on the work of others, whereas the better half of my faith in God is based upon my experience. I have felt Him; I have seen things in my life so obvious, and so clear, that they afford no other explanation apart from God. The greatest of these is the amazing way in which He has changed my life. If I were to think five years ago that I'd be writing a book advocating the worth of investigating Christianity and its Truth, I'd be overcome with shock, or laughter.

Faith is a choice. It is something we choose based upon knowledge obtained from others and personal experience. Will you choose to learn more about Jesus? Will you choose to believe in Him? Will you seek out God, and learn of His love for you, and the gifts He longs to give you? Will you do the research?

PART II
ଔ
RESOURCES

"Entrust the past to God's mercy, the present to His love, the future to His providence."
-St. Augustine

SEVEN

☙

DOING THE RESEARCH

―――――――――

"Ancora imparo." (I am still learning.)
-Michelangelo

CHRISTIANITY 101

So let me ask you, have you decided to stay on board and really start to have some fun? That's right, this is going to be fun. This isn't like the book report you had to do in school; this is a journey of the self, done at your own pace. Researching Christianity is interesting, exhilarating, and rewarding. I am sure you will enjoy it. I have devoted this entire final chapter to equipping you in the best way I can, so you may hit the ground running.

Before you go searching for answers, I would like to recommend three things to you, in order of importance:

First, remember that seeking out Christ is a heavenly pursuit. A holy life isn't what happens after reading a few good books or attending church every week. Rather, it is the result of a loving relationship with Jesus Christ, and the work He does in your heart. Your love for God, and your walk with Him, is what will lead you to a godly life. Let's not forget about God's love for *you*, either! Doing the research, and taking up the earthly chase necessary to answer your questions about Christianity is a step in the right direction, but the pursuit of holiness does not end once you believe; it begins.

Secondly, I would like to present a word of caution: you are never going to get all of your questions answered. One of the things that you will need to accept sooner or later is that there are some things that we humans just don't know, and never will know while we are on this side of eternity. However, we can take solace in the fact that God has provided us with all we *need* to know. There will be unanswered questions and there will be things that force us to hypothesize, but rest assured that if God wanted us to know a certain fact, He would present it to us, assuming we were capable of understanding it. There isn't a doctrine in the world that has everything explained down to the last detail. Though it may be humbling, as finite, limited human beings, we must learn to accept that there will be unanswered questions in our lives. Take heart. Trust God.

"If God wanted us to know a certain fact, He would present it to us."

Third, I recommend that you understand your questions before you search for answers. As I mentioned earlier in this book, many people disagree with the Christian faith in ignorance. Despite a Catholic upbringing, I myself didn't truly understand what being a Christian meant until I was twenty-five. As a first order of business, I would recommend finding out what Christians believe. The next section addresses this topic specifically.

Before continuing, permit me to give you one final, gentle push: **start now**. Do not wait any longer than you have to before starting your journey. Our nation's bookstores and libraries are stockpiled with thousands of books aimed at motivating you to take some sort of action in your life. From diets to the latest in leadership development, none of them are worth a dime to you if you don't take any action after you read them. This book is no exception.

Folks in the business world refer to this as the law of "diminishing intent." In simpler terms it means that the longer you wait to take action on a certain decision, the less likely you are to follow through with it. Your intent to take action will diminish with time.

There is a humorous story about three frogs sitting on a log: one of the frogs makes a decision to jump into the water. How many frogs remain on the log? The answer is three. Making a decision to jump into the water isn't worth much until the frog actually does it.

I can read a book about the numerous health benefits of exercise, and finish it feeling a surge of motivation to start working out regularly. Perhaps this has happened to you. If well written, the book will convince me that I need to make exercise a part of my life if I wish to enjoy a healthy physical existence. I'll be sold all the way, just itching to take a jog...for about a day. Then, slowly, as the natural business of my life takes over, my enthusiasm for beginning an exercise regimen will fade. Before I'm aware of it, a month will have passed without my having run a single mile, and I'll wonder why I was so excited about exercise in the first place. In no time, I'm back to where I started.

"The longer you wait to take action on a certain decision, the less likely you are to follow through with it."

Such is the case with this book. If I've been even moderately successful, and you have found yourself agreeing with me at any point during this book in that you owe it to yourself to explore Christianity, I urge you, start now. You do not have to rush once you've begun, but you must begin soon, before this book gets shelved along with any enthusiasm you may have for its message. All of the power is in your hands: you can easily shrug this off, wait until tomorrow, or next week. What is your choice? For best results, I recommend starting as soon as you are capable.

WHAT CHRISTIANS BELIEVE (ABRIDGED VERSION)

At the most fundamental level, Christians believe in the truth of the Bible. The Bible contains the perfect Word of God, and everything we need to know about living our lives on earth. I once heard actor Gary Bussey joke that the word "Bible" is an acronym for "Basic Instructions Before Leaving Earth." Though this is true, and rather cute, the Bible is so much more.

From belief in the Bible, we may sum up what lies at the center of the Christian faith:

1) *We are sinners, and have thus separated ourselves from God.*

God has given each human being free will. We are not puppets! God wishes for us to love and obey Him, because He loves us. For love and obedience to be sincere, they must be chosen. God could have easily created a bunch of robots that loved Him unconditionally, but then it wouldn't have truly been love. He could also force obedience upon us, but we're not really being obedient then, are we? Thus, each human being makes a choice to love and obey God, or to do otherwise.

"Doing otherwise" is called sin. By sinning, we chose something other than God. In so doing, we are no longer right in His eyes. We have fallen short of the perfection that is God. We distance ourselves from Him.

Why did God give us all of these rules to follow? Because He loves us. God's commandments are for our own good. They aren't volumes of thorny laws designed to make us suffer, or live a life of misery. They are for our benefit.

When I was younger, my brother and I would always put up a fight at night when our parents told us it was time for bed. I think most of you can identify with this. We didn't want to go to bed! We wanted to stay up! Furthermore, we couldn't understand why we had to go to bed early. We weren't even tired!

Our parents won the argument of course, and we would be tucked in promptly at eight o'clock each night. Why did my parents do this? Simple: because it was for our own good. We were young, growing children, and needed a good night's rest. In addition, the discipline of going to bed early reinforced the respect we had for our parents. It emphasized their authority in our lives. In the end, it strengthened our relationship with them.

"God's commandments are for our own good."

In a similar manner, all of God's "rules" are for our benefit, and strengthen our relationship with Him. If the entire world followed God's commands to the letter, do you think we would all be miserable and suffering? Or do you think we might live in a better place?

Did God tell us "Do not commit adultery" because He wanted to deny us the pleasure of sex? No way. Adultery destroys marriages, spreads disease, breaks up families, and creates unwanted children. Are any of these things good for people? Of course not! That's why God forbids adulterous relationships.

2) *The price of sin is death, and eternal separation from God.*

There is a price to be paid if we choose other than

God's will for us. This is death, and eternal separation from God. Why? Isn't that cruel? If God loved us, He'd let us slide, right? Remember, God is perfect. He is 100% free of any evil or imperfection. He is also the epitome of love, truth, and justice. God is also unchanging. He is, was, and will be all of these things forever.

How then, can we be with God in Heaven if we are not perfect as He is? If we harbor sinful desires and evil thoughts, we fall short of God's glory. If He let us slide, then He wouldn't be just, would He? If I commit a crime, and the judge lets me off with no punishment, justice has not been served. God is not a pushover. Sin is very serious to Him, as it should be to us. When we sin, we reject God. That's a big deal. There isn't any place in Heaven for people who are just "okay." There is no "good enough" for Heaven. There can be no imperfection in a place of total perfection.

"When we sin, we reject God."

3) Jesus Christ paid the price for our sins once and for all.

Now, the Good News, also known as the Gospel: God became man in Jesus Christ, and paid the price of our sins for us! Consider the courtroom analogy again: I'm on trial for speeding. I'm found guilty and fined $200. The judge bangs his gavel; justice has been served. I must pay for my wrongdoing. After the trial, the judge takes off his robe, pulls out his wallet, and pays the $200 for me. Now I am restored in the eyes of the law, and may go, free of any debt.

This is what God has done for us through Jesus. As a true, fair, and just God, He finds us guilty of our sins, and we are convicted. We are sentenced to death. God then becomes one of us, and pays our sentence: He suffers and dies a horrible death. Three days later, He rises from the grave, victorious over sin and death. Now we are restored, and free to enjoy eternal life in His presence.

A common question here is, "Why does a price have to be paid at all? Why can't God just forgive us?" God does forgive us, but a price must be paid for our sins. Forgiveness demands a price. As a child, I once broke one of my father's tools. Because he loved me, my father forgave me. The broken tool, however, remained broken. My father paid that price by forgiving me: he either suffered without the tool, or bought a new one. Forgiveness always costs, and it cost God the ultimate price: His Son. He loves us that much.

4) By believing in Jesus, our relationship with God is restored, and we may be saved.

Salvation, then, is a gift from God. We are saved by God's grace, and God's grace alone. We do not, and cannot, earn it in any way. If we wish to be saved, and have our record wiped clean, we must believe in Jesus. We must receive Him as our personal savior, and trust in Him alone for forgiveness.

As I've mentioned before, like any gift, we must receive salvation. I could have pushed away the $200 the judge was offering for my speeding ticket. In the same way, we must receive the gift of salvation through Jesus. God is here right now, offering us His gift. All we have to do is receive it.

"We are saved by God's grace, and God's grace alone."

How do we receive it? You can do it at any time, in any place. All you need to do is pray (i.e., talk) to God. A simple prayer of faith is all you need to accept Christ, and receive salvation:

Lord God, I know that I am a sinner, and have sinned against You in my thoughts, words and deeds. I am sorry for my sins, and choose to turn away from them now. I believe that Jesus died for my sins, and I pray right now for Your forgiveness through Him. Please come into my life and change my heart. I want to follow You and know You better. Help me to forsake my sins, and follow You always. I pray in Jesus' name. Amen.

For a more detailed explanation of this prayer, with references to scripture, Billy Graham has an excellent web site at www.billygraham.org. Here, Mr. Graham presents the main thrust of mankind's relationship with God, why it is broken, and how Jesus fixes it. Also included are answers to questions asked by readers. I highly recommend this site as a good starting point.

WHAT WOULD YOU LIKE TO KNOW?

When I was first learning about the Christian religion, I would write down questions I had, so I could remember to look them up or ask somebody at a later time. This proved to be a very useful method for hashing out some of my concerns. Before really digging in, take some time to jot down what you think is keeping you from believing. Perhaps you can start by answering the question, "why don't I believe?" Here is what my list of questions might have looked like some years ago:

1. Is the Bible accurate? Can I trust it? How do I know? Does archeology confirm or deny Biblical events? Isn't the Bible full of contradictions?
2. Did Jesus literally rise up from the dead, or is it

just a figurative expression? Was Jesus really the Son of God? Was He really born of a virgin?
3. Does God really exist? Do miracles really happen? Why won't God perform a miracle for me, so I will believe?
4. Christianity seems close-minded. How could there just be one *way to salvation? What if I'm a good person? Is sincerity enough?*

The information available on Christianity is nothing short of overwhelming. I would recommend focusing on questions concerning Jesus first. The life and teachings of Jesus are the keys to Christianity (no surprise there). Belief in the Gospels (that is, the first four books in the New Testament: Matthew, Mark, Luke, and John) provides the foundation for everything else.

Questions about evolution or why God allows suffering in the world are among the most popular among nonbelievers. Though very important, they aren't as crucial to the center of Christianity as Jesus is. Focus on Him first, then use your list of questions to help you decide where to go next.

In the next few sections, I present an inkling of the wealth of information available to you that can answer your questions. As you explore, please remember that everybody is different. For some, it may take only one book to convince them of the validity of Christianity. For others, it may take years of reading and soul-searching. Some learn best from books, others need one on one conversation, still others prefer the internet. The journey is different for all, but the destination is the same.

"God will be on your side."

Please remember to be patient, but most of all, be persistent. There are many forces out in the world that do not want you to succeed on this mission. Remember to always be true to yourself, and you will never fail. Also, believe in Him or not, God will be on your side, helping you along. I pray that you find your research to be both enjoyable and edifying. If you stick with it, I can almost guarantee you will.

CHRISTIAN TREE PULP

I recommend beginning your research at a bookstore. A Christian bookstore is all the better. The branch of theology devoted to the defense of Christianity is known as apologetics. This might be a useful keyword to help you get started when you're at a bookstore or web site. Any reading is good reading, in my mind, but here are a few books of which I am particularly fond:

1.) ***Know Why You Believe*** by Paul E. Little.
   This was the first book I ever read which tackled the big questions I had about Christianity: Is there really a God? Did Jesus really rise from the dead? Is the Bible really accurate? As this was the first book to really get me thinking, it still holds a special place in my heart.
2.) ***A Ready Defense*** by Josh McDowell.
   This book is the mother lode. In actuality, it is a compilation of twelve books authored and co-authored by Mr. McDowell. I find it very useful as a reference book. Find your question du jour in the table of contents, and look it up. A wealth of material is covered, and quite well. Mr. McDowell also maintains a web site at www.josh.org, and has authored many excellent apologetic books.
3.) ***The Screwtape Letters*** by C.S. Lewis.
   Though a work of fiction, this is a fantastic book written by one of the world's most renowned Christian authors. The book consists of a series of letters from a

demon, Screwtape, to his nephew, Wormwood. As servants of Satan, the elder tempter advises his younger nephew how to best lead his "patient" away from the Lord. It provides many insights into the numerous ways we may be led away from the Truth. Also by C.S. Lewis is his acclaimed *Mere Christianity*, which provides a compelling case for Christianity with the logic and writing acumen that make Mr. Lewis one of my favorite authors.

4.) ***The Case For Christ*** by Lee Strobel.

In this book, the award winning Yale-educated journalist and former atheist Lee Strobel sets out to determine if there is credible evidence for believing that Jesus of Nazareth is the Son of God. Also written by Strobel is ***The Case for Faith***, which sets out to answer some of the most common Christian questions, such as "why does God allow suffering?"

Understand that I barely scratch the surface of what's available with these few books. I've simply chosen a few above that might be good places to get your gears turning, but there are literally hundreds from which you may choose. Books are available on every subject, for readers of just about every level. Some Christian books stores will even have small flyers and pamphlets that summarize important concepts. Other authors that I would highly recommend are Charles Colson, Billy Graham, David Jerimiah, Erwin Lutzer, Charles Stanley, Charles Swindoll, and Philip Yancey.

Eventually, you may want to purchase a Bible. This can be a task all its own! The Bible consists of sixty-six different books divided into two segments: The Old Testament (before the birth of Jesus) and The New Testament (after the birth of Jesus). When you buy a Bible, you are really purchasing a translation. The Bible actually resides on ancient Hebrew and Greek texts. A Bible translation is a process that takes the dedication of numerous scholars, experts, and theologians many years to complete.

Several English translations are available in bookstores today: the King James Version, the New International Version, Today's English Version, and the New Living Translation name a handful.[16] Depending on when the translation was written, you may find some easier to understand than others. In my opinion, one of the best translations to begin with is the New Living Translation. I personally find this to be the most readable of all the translations available.

Many publishers make what's called a study Bible in several translations. I highly recommend such a Bible to anybody interested in better understanding this important book. Study Bibles provide a wealth of notes about the text, which shed greater light on its meaning. Also included are biographies of important people mentioned in The Bible, maps of key locations, and summaries of each book.

CHRISTIAN ELECTRONS

Here are some of the web sites that I have bookmarked:

www.billygraham.org. Billy Graham didn't become one of the world's most renowned evangelists by dodging the issues. I believe this site to be a great starting point to understanding the Christian faith, and finding answers to tough questions.

www.christiananswers.net. The name says it all!

---

[16] A translation I would definitely *not* recommend is the "New World Translation" of the Bible. This is the "Bible" used by the Jehovah's Witnesses, a dangerous cult. The New World Translation contains numerous alterations to the original text that have been incorporated to keep consistent with their distorted view of Christ.

This site has hundreds of frequently asked questions and their answers. I highly recommend this web site as another good place to start answering your questions. This site covers everything from contemporary issues like abortion, to the most fundamental questions involving Jesus and the Bible.

www.carm.org. "CARM" stands for "Christian Apologetics and Research Ministry," and has numerous resources, as well as excellent material on its web site. One section of the page contains "40 Objections" that non-Christians typically have to Christianity, and potential answers.

www.christianity.org. This is a large site, which has hundreds of links to other Christian related web pages.

www.exanimopress.com. This is my publisher's website, which has links to the sites mentioned above, as well as many other resources.

CHRISTIAN PEOPLE

I've saved the best for last! There are millions of Christians in the world who would love to speak about their faith with you. Nothing can answer your questions as well as an interactive conversation with a live person. Though it may be uncomfortable at first, having a spiritual mentor, or "answer person" can become a tremendous blessing, as it was for me with my friend Randy. Seek out a local church where the Bible is taught and make an effort to become familiar with the people there. Most good churches will have Bible study classes, as well as missionary programs.

"Seek out a local church where the Bible is taught."

I should mention, however, that although this is probably the best means of gathering information, it could also be the most dangerous. There are people today who still misuse the teachings of the Bible. Whether by intent or accident, being led astray can be very damaging to you spiritually. The most effective way to guard yourself against this is with knowledge. If you're just starting out, this can make you very vulnerable.

I don't mean to frighten you into thinking that evil "Christians" are waiting to lead you to spiritual ruin at every corner. Just remember that Satan doesn't want to lose you, and his chief weapon is deceit. Follow your conscience in such matters. People who pressure you into commitment, or make any unreasonable demands right away are probably not followers of Christ. At best, they are struggling to find peace with their faith themselves, and may not make the best mentors.

Examining a religion's views on Jesus serves as the litmus test for cults, or other supposed "Christian" religions. Any doctrine that portrays Jesus as anything *less* than the only begotten Son of God, both fully human and fully God, who lived a sinless life, died and rose from the dead to pay for our sins is *not* Christian!

Some of the more prevalent cults in today's society include: Mormonism, Jehovah's Witnesses, Unification Church, Christian Science, Armstrongism, and Unity School of Christianity. Be wary also of the "Faith Movement" and its teachers.[17] Members of these cults may profess many Christian beliefs, such as belief in one God, and even in the Bible. Members may be loving, kind, generous, and truly sincere in their belief and desire to help you. At best, they too are deceived by Satan's lies. Cults deceive

"A religion's view on Jesus serves as the litmus test for cults."

---

[17] You can read more about The Faith Movement (or Faith-Word Movement) in Hank Hanegraaff's book, *Christianity in Crisis*.

millions of men and women, often leading them to spiritual ruin. If you are new to Christianity, I would strongly discourage engaging in a religious discussion with any men or women who are members of these cults.

Ask a trusted Christian friend what church they attend. Most of all, don't be afraid to introduce yourself to others in the church, especially the pastor or priest. The Christian faith is a missionary faith, and most people will be eager to meet you and help you along. Many churches have special classes and meetings for new believers or seekers. These are golden opportunities for new or potential Christians to learn more about the faith. Chances are you'll make some good friends along the way, too.

Epilogue

Have you ever had a truly fantastic experience that you couldn't wait to share with others? I'm sure you have. Maybe it was a restaurant you ate at, a book you read (...ahem...) or a movie you watched. After that experience, did you find yourself acting as an evangelist? Did you want to tell the world about your experience in the hopes that they could share in your happiness?

Evangelism doesn't just refer to people asking for money on television. In fact, that's not evangelism at all. I prefer to think of evangelism in a very broad sense. An evangelist, in my mind, is a type of salesperson. The difference is that evangelists don't really want to sell a product. They're trying to sell an experience, or something revolutionary. "You gotta go see this movie!" "You have to try the salmon at this restaurant!"

> *"Evangelists advocate their belief simply because they think it is a better way."*

Another key difference is that true evangelists don't receive any benefit from a successful sale. If I recommend a movie to you, and you see it, I have nothing to gain other than your thanks, assuming you enjoy it. Evangelists advocate their belief simply because they think it is a better way, which is for the benefit and enjoyment of all.

In the same way, I consider myself an evangelist. I have experienced the joy and peace of knowing Christ, and I want the whole world to know it as well. Furthermore, in the Bible, Jesus commands his followers to spread the Good News. I therefore consider my effort here obedient at best, but certainly not heroic or noble. Without doubt, this book has been one of the most difficult things for me to finish. Each day I would come across another example, analogy, quotation, argument or rebuttal that I would consider recording here. However, I personally hold that an exhaustive discourse on the merit of researching Christianity, or of the Truth of Christianity itself, is impossible.

No single book could possibly contain everything, and despite the most excellent arguments of Christianity's best and brightest, a person's decision to accept or reject Christ ultimately comes down to a personal choice in his or her own heart. It is always a personal matter. Though writers may stimulate, and preachers pontificate, it is always God who does the work in the end. God is the one who softens your heart. God is the one who meets you exactly where you are. God is the one who saves you.

> *"No single book could possibly contain everything."*

I encourage you to write to my publisher and tell me about your experience before, during or after this book. I would love to hear from you. I hope that someday I will receive letters detailing testimonials 19,948,342,645 and beyond. Either way, I wish you nothing but God's best as you walk through life. You are in my prayers each night. May you come to know Jesus Christ personally, and may His peace and love be with you always.

ATTRIBUTIONS

Chapter 3
The excerpt from *My Utmost for His Highest* by Oswald Chambers. © 1935 by Dodd Mead & Co., renewed © 1963 by the Oswald Chambers Publications Assn. Ltd., and is used by permission of Discovery House Publishers, Box 3566, Grand Rapids MI 49501. All rights reserved.

Chapter 5
The excerpt from Billy Graham's "My Answer": © Tribune Media Services, Inc. All rights reserved. Reprinted with permission.

Chapter 6
The excerpt from the book, *Alcoholics Anonymous*, is reprinted with permission of Alcoholics Anonymous World Services, Inc. (AAWS). Permission to reprint this excerpt does not mean that A.A.W.S. has reviewed or approved the contents of this publication, or that A.A.W.S. necessarily agrees with the views expressed herein. A.A. is a program of recovery from alcoholism only – use of this excerpt in connection with programs and activities which are patterned after A.A., but which address other problems, or in any other non A.A. context, does not imply otherwise. Although Alcoholics Anonymous is a spiritual program, A.A. is not a religious program, and use of A.A. material in the present connection does not imply A.A.'s affiliation with or endorsement of, any sect, denomination, or specific religious belief.

Quick Order Form

Telephone orders: Call 1-866-634-0788 toll free.
Web orders: Visit www.exanimopress.com
e-mail orders: orders@exanimopress.com
Postal orders: Ex Animo Press, Inc., 430 Franklin Village Drive, Suite 167a, Franklin, MA 02038-4007, USA
Price: $10.95 (U.S. Dollars only) per book.
Sales tax: Please add 5% sales tax for books shipped to Massachusetts addresses.
Shipping and handling
U.S. & Canada: $3.95 for first book, add $1.00 for each additional book. $9.95 for orders of 10 books or more.

Please send _____ **copies of** *Permissive Ignorance* **to:**
Name:_____
Address:_____
City:_____ State:_____ Zip:_____
Telephone (optional): (_____) _____ - _____
e-mail address:_____
___ Please add me to your mailing list
___ Please send me information about speaking engagements

Payment:
___ Check or money order (enclosed)   ___ Visa
___ MasterCard   ___ AMEX   ___ Discover

Card number:_____
Name on card:_____ Exp. Date:_____